Versailles and After 1919–1933

IN THE SAME SERIES

General Editors: Eric J. Evans and P.D. King

LANCASTER PAMPHLETS

Versailles and after
1919–1933

Ruth Henig

London and New York

First published 1984
by Methuen & Co. Ltd

Second edition first published 1995
by Routledge
2 Park Square, Milton Park, Abingdon, Oxon, OX14 4RN

Simultaneously published in the USA and Canada
by Routledge
270 Madison Ave, New York NY 10016

Reprinted 1997

Transferred to Digital Printing 2005

© *1995 Ruth Henig*

Typeset in Bembo by
Ponting–Green Publishing Services, Chesham, Bucks

British Library Cataloguing in Publication Data
A catalogue record for this book is available from the British Library

Library of Congress Cataloguing in Publication Data
Henig, Ruth B. (Ruth Beatrice)
Versailles and after, 1919–1933 / Ruth Henig. – 2nd ed.
p.   cm. – (Lancaster Pamphlets)
Includes bibliographical references.
1. Treaty of Versailles (1919)
2. World War, 1914–1918–Peace.
3. World War, 1914–1918–United States.
4. League of Nations–History.
I. Title.   II. Series.
D643.A7H43   1995
940.3'142–dc20   94–41756

ISBN 0–415–12710–6

Contents

Foreword

Lancaster Pamphlets offer concise and up-to-date accounts of major historical topics, primarily for the help of students preparing for Advanced Level examinations, though they should also be of value to those pursuing introductory courses in universities and other institutions of higher education. They do not rely on prior textbook knowledge. Without being all-embracing, their aims are to bring some of the central themes or problems confronting students and teachers into sharper focus than the textbook writer can hope to do; to provide the reader with some of the results of recent research which the textbook may not embody; and to stimulate thought about the whole interpretation of the topic under discussion. They are written by experienced university scholars who have a strong interest in teaching.

Acknowledgements

I would like to take this opportunity of thanking my colleagues Dr E. J. Evans and Dr P. D. King for their careful scrutiny of the text and for their valuable suggestions concerning both content and presentation. Thanks are also due to all former students of my Special Subject option, 'British Foreign Policy, 1919–33', who have contributed wittingly or unwittingly to the writing of this pamphlet. It is dedicated to my two sons, Simon and David, who, in recent years, have not had as much of my time and attention as they would have liked. I hope they may find it useful in the years ahead.

Ruth Henig
January 1995

Chronology of events

1915

April   Treaty of London brings Italy into war on allied side; in same negotiations, Russia promised Constantinople and Straits if Turkey defeated
In Far East, Japan forces concessions from China by way of Twenty-one Demands

1915–16

Letters exchanged between British High Commissioner in Egypt and Sherif of Mecca to encourage Arab revolt against Turks in Middle East. Arabs promised their own state

1916

Sykes/Picot agreement divides up Turkish empire in Asia between Britain, France and Russia
November Woodrow Wilson re-elected as United States President. Promises to make world 'safe for democracy'

1917

February/ March	Tsarist regime falls in Russia
April	Agreement at St Jean de Maurienne between Britain, France and Italy gives Italy a sphere of influence in Near East; United States enters war to 'save democracy' Britain and Japan agree to support each other in dividing up Germany's Pacific possessions; United States acknowledges Japanese claims to nearby territories
October/ November	Bolsheviks seize power in Russia
November	Balfour Declaration promises Jews a national home in Palestine

1918

January	Wilson delivers 'Fourteen Points' speech to United States Congress
March	Treaty of Brest-Litovsk between Germany and Russia takes Russia out of First World War
4 October	German government seeks armistice on basis of Wilson's 'Fourteen Points'
5 November	United States and Allies agree to armistice based on 'Fourteen Points' but with reservations to Points 2 and 7; Republican party gains majority in United States Congress in mid-term elections
11 November	Armistice signed between Germany and allies; Clemenceau: 'we have won the war, now we have to win the peace'
December	British general election results in victory for Lloyd George. Electorate clamour to 'make Germany pay' for war

1919

winter–spring	Europe-wide flu epidemic claims millions of lives
January	Paris peace conference starts
14 February	delegates reach agreement on a League of Nations
late February	Wilson returns to United States to face mounting criticism from Congress
March	Council of Four established at Paris to thrash out most contentious issues
May	Treaty of Versailles handed to German representatives; Germans make lengthy written criticisms
June	German high seas fleet is scuttled at Scapa Flow
28 June	Treaty of Versailles with Germans signed in Hall of Mirrors, Versailles
10 September	Treaty of St Germain signed with Austria
27 November	Treaty of Neuilly signed with Bulgaria

1920

10 January	Treaty of Versailles, and League of Nations come into force
March	Allenstein, Marienwerder vote in plebiscite to be part of Germany; Russo-Polish conflict – ended by Treaty of Riga
19 March	Final attempt to ratify Treaty of Versailles in United States Senate fails. United States subsequently signs separate peace treaty with Germany
4 June	Treaty of Trianon signed with Hungary
10 August	Treaty of Sèvres signed with Turkish empire League solves Aland Islands dispute between Sweden and Finland

1921

January	allied conference sets Germany's reparations bill at 132 billion German marks

February	France and Poland sign alliance treaty with secret military convention
March	French occupy some German towns in Ruhr because of refusal of Germany to comply fully with Treaty of Versailles
	League of Nations supervises partition of Upper Silesia between Germany and Poland
1921–2	Washington Conference draws up naval treaty limiting capital ships of Britain, United States, Japan, France and Italy; Four-Power pact between United States, Japan, Britain and France replaces Anglo-Japanese alliance

1922

March	Genoa conference on disarmament and economic recovery of Europe convenes; its only outcome is Treaty of Rapallo, signed between Germany and Russia on 15 April
September	Chanak crisis brings Turkish troops to brink of war with Britain in Near East
30 October	Mussolini comes to power in Italy

1923

	Treaty of Lausanne finally brings peace between allies and new nationalist government of Turkey
January	Belgian and French troops invade Ruhr to force Germany to pay reparations due. Leads to collapse of German currency and massive inflation
September	Italy seizes Corfu; League and Conference of Ambassadors work together to solve crisis

1924

January	France and Czechoslovakia sign alliance, but with no secret military convention
August	with help of United States, Dawes plan agreed – lays down reduced schedule of German reparations payments

xiv

September–October	League of Nations draws up Geneva Protocol – rejected by new British Conservative government

1925

	military conflict between Greece and Bulgaria averted by League
October	mutual security pact signed at Locarno. Frontiers between Belgium, Germany and France agreed to by all three powers France begins to build Maginot line along frontier with Germany

1926

May	Preparatory Disarmament Commission starts work in Geneva
September	League of Nations votes to accept Germany as a member

1928

	Kellogg-Briand pact (also known as Pact of Paris) drawn up: signatories agree to renounce war in their pursuit of national interests

1929

June	Young plan for reparations payments replaces Dawes plan
October	Wall Street crash triggers off Great Depression

1930

	London naval conference – results in limitation of cruisers as between United States, Japan and Britain
June	last occupation troops leave Rhineland, five years ahead of schedule

September	In German national elections, Nazi party makes sweeping gains
1931	
September	Japanese troops invade Manchuria
1932	
	reparations payments suspended by Lausanne conference; League report into Manchurian crisis, drawn up by Lord Lytton, ignored by Japanese. They announce intention to leave League in two years
February	Fifty-nine states attend opening of League of Nations Disarmament Conference
1933	
January	Hitler becomes Chancellor of Germany
October	Germany withdraws from Disarmament Conference and announces intention to leave League of Nations

Western and Central Europe in 1919

Versailles and After
1919–1933

Introduction

In January 1919 the leaders of thirty-two countries, repre-
senting between them some three-quarters of the world's population, assembled in Paris. Just two months previously, after four
years of unremitting and savage conflict, an armistice had finally
brought the First World War to its end. Now the politicians had
to grapple with a whole range of problems thrown up by the
war, and to thrash out the terms of a peace settlement. Their task
was one of formidable complexity and difficulty, in view of the
intractable nature of the issues to be resolved and the number of
seemingly contradictory viewpoints and aspirations to be recon-
ciled. In the circumstances, the settlement that emerged from the
months of deliberation at Paris was a creditable achievement.
The fact that it did not survive the 1920s intact stemmed, as we
shall see, not so much from the terms of the peace treaties
themselves but from the reluctance of political leaders in the
inter-war period to enforce them.

Shaping the peace

Public opinion in the allied countries
One of the most important factors influencing the shape of the
peace settlement was the strength of popular feeling in Britain,

1

Italy and, more particularly, the countries invaded by German troops during the war: France and Belgium. To explain this, we need do no more than consider the unprecedented nature of the recent conflict. The First World War was fought on a scale, and at a cost in human suffering, unparalleled in the history of mankind. Countries from every continent, including most of those in Europe, had taken part. New weapons, such as aeroplanes, submarines and tanks, had widened the scope and sharpened the impact of warfare. Whole populations had been marshalled to serve their countries' war efforts. More than 10 million people had lost their lives, and millions more endured maiming, gassing, malnutrition, impoverishment or uprooting from their homes. Even as the delegates met at Paris, Europe lay in the grip of an influenza epidemic which claimed probably some 40 million lives and which unquestionably owed much of its devastating impact to the lowered resistance of its victims, stemming from the long years of the war. Such was the magnitude of the sacrifices which the principal protagonists had been called upon to make, and such was the closeness of civilian involvement in the struggle, that it was inevitable that emotions would run high. In Britain and France in particular, a strong current of opinion looked to the peace-makers to lay the blame for the war where it belonged, with Germany, and to exact punishment, including the surrender of territory, from the nation seen as being responsible for so much bloodshed and misery. There were many voices demanding that the Kaiser himself should be hanged. But alongside the call for retribution went the cry that never again should people have to endure the horrors of modern warfare. In France, this reinforced the demands for a punitive peace that would prevent Germany from waging war in the future. In Britain, however, some saw the prevention of future wars as a general problem that could only be tackled by the setting up of an international body to keep the peace.

Another demand which was strongly voiced was summed up in the words of the First Lord of the Admiralty, Eric Geddes: that the victorious allies should 'squeeze the German lemon until the pips squeak'. Economically, the impact of the war had been devastating. It is estimated to have cost in the region of £45,000 million, and had inflicted grave damage upon the leading industrial nations of Europe. Those who had been involved in the fighting from the outset had been obliged to gear their economies to serve military needs, and had been forced to relinquish many of their lucrative overseas markets to their non-European competitors – notably to Japan, which played only a peripheral role in the fighting, and to the United States, which entered the war only in 1917. European countries which had managed to remain neutral during the war had suffered along with belligerent nations from the consequences of the crucial struggle for control of the seas, which involved German submarine attacks on merchant shipping and a British blockade of German ports. At the end of the war, the need to rebuild the economies of the leading European powers as swiftly as possible was widely recognized by economic experts and government officials, especially in Britain. But European governments had met the enormous costs of war largely by raising loans – from their own nationals, from bankers, and above all from American financiers. As hostilities dragged on, and as the amounts borrowed soared steeply, so the goal of victory had come increasingly to be associated with the prospect of redeeming those debts by the recouping of costs from the defeated enemy. Clearly, the demand for full reparations was not reconcilable with the desire for general economic reconstruction in Europe. Public opinion in Britain and France, however, whether motivated by sentiments of revenge or a conviction that reparations were no more than just, was firmly in favour of making Germany pay.

The popular press had developed during the war into a major influence on the formation of public opinion. With leading articles and features focusing on various war issues, often presented in grossly over-simplified terms, it played its part in raising the temperature of attitude and debate. It also ensured that the peace-makers at Paris, unlike their counter-parts at Vienna a hundred years previously, or at Utrecht two hundred years before, had to negotiate in the full glare of publicity, knowing that details of their discussions would be carried the next day in newspaper columns throughout the world.

The presence in Paris of hundreds of journalists merely underlined the fact that the freedom of negotiation of allied leaders was circumscribed by their accountability to their electorates. The principal peace-makers were aware that, as the

3

leaders of democratic nations, they would have to answer for their decisions to their electorates. Indeed, Lloyd George, the British Prime Minister, came to the Paris peace conference shortly after an election which left him in no doubt whatsoever as to the voters' wishes. The election campaign which began in Britain in November 1918 was the first since 1910, and the first to be conducted on the basis of full manhood suffrage and a limited franchise for women. Although Lloyd George was seen as the architect of victory, the deep split which had divided the Liberal ranks in the course of the war ensured that he was not in a sufficiently strong political position to go to the country on his own terms. Instead, he secured the support of the Conservatives and of a small section of the Labour party for the perpetuation of the war coalition and a policy of making Germany pay for the war. The large majorities by which Lloyd George's coalition supporters were returned to power in December demonstrated that this was exactly what the new mass electorate wanted. The campaign had been a heated one, with vociferous and widespread calls for a punitive settlement, and those candidates who had espoused the very different principles of the Wilsonian peace programme (see Appendix Two) had found great difficulty in making themselves heard.

If Lloyd George knew that his political future depended upon the maintenance of a hard line towards Germany, so too did the French Prime Minister, Clemenceau. After the war the French Chamber of Deputies was nicknamed 'the one-legged chamber' because of the number of maimed ex-soldiers it contained. These men would be satisfied with nothing less than a punitive peace, and they had a doughty champion in Marshal Foch, allied commander-in-chief during the final stages of the war, who was present at the Paris peace negotiations and could be relied upon to ensure that Clemenceau did not moderate his stance. Similar sentiments inspired the Italians, who looked to the peace treaties to give them the great territorial and economic gains which would compensate them for their heavy losses in the war and would make Italy at last into the great power they yearned for her to be. Orlando, the Italian Prime Minister, was well aware that if he failed to deliver the goods he would be charged with betrayal by more extreme nationalist elements seeking to expand their political influence.

4

The case of Italy is a reminder that the peace-makers at Paris had also to take into account a number of commitments which had been entered into as a result of the heavy economic and military costs of the war. The more protracted the war, the larger was the number of secret diplomatic agreements entered into by the various participants. Sometimes the undertakings they embodied were in conflict with each other; more often, they involved the disposition of territory long in contention or the concession of economic advantage long coveted. When the full extent of the secret wartime diplomacy was revealed, and the beneficiaries called in their debts at the peace negotiations, much bitterness and argument ensued.

Italy was one such beneficiary. A pre-war ally of Germany and Austria-Hungary, she had not only declined to enter the war in their support but in May 1915 had agreed to join Britain, France and Russia against them. The price of her entry was set out in the secret Treaty of London, signed by all four nations on 26 April 1915. In addition to somewhat vague assurances that she would receive a 'just share' in any partition of the Ottoman empire and further territory if Britain and France annexed any German colonies, Italy was promised sovereignty over the Dodecanese islands (which she was already occupying) and major territorial gains at the expense of the Habsburg empire: to her north, the German-speaking Alpine regions of the Trentino and South Tyrol, and, across the Adriatic Sea, Istria and part of Dalmatia, both Slav-populated. If these specific promises materialized, almost a quarter of a million German-speaking Austrians and well over half a million Slavs and Turks would find themselves incorporated into the Italian kingdom. Such a transfer of populations would not only weaken Austria-Hungary very severely and threaten the establishment of a strong Serbia and a stable Albania; it would also run completely counter to any attempt to reorganize Europe after the war on lines of national self-determination. Lloyd George remarked ruefully of these Italian diplomatic gains that 'war plays havoc with the refinements of conscience'. Italy's presentation of her bill for payment at the end of the war was to pose major problems for the peace-makers.

The collapse of Tsarist Russia in 1917, and Bolshevik repudiation of the secret wartime agreements entered into, saved

Britain and France from the consequences of the most far-reaching commitment which they made, also in 1915, namely the promise to Russia of Constantinople and the Dardanelles Straits. Throughout the nineteenth century, Britain and France had striven to deny Russian ships access to the Mediterranean through this region. Wartime pressures forced a dramatic change of policy, but the Tsar did not survive long enough to claim his coveted prize. Other agreements relating to the Ottoman empire remained to be enforced or modified at the end of the war. In correspondence with the Sherif of Mecca in 1915 and early 1916, Britain's High Commissioner in Egypt, Sir Henry McMahon, had promised that Britain would recognize and support the independence of the Arabs in all regions demanded by the Sherif, save for the coastal strip west of the line Damascus–Hama–Homs–Aleppo and save for areas where Britain was not free to act without detriment to French interests. No specific mention was made of Palestine. The partition of the Ottoman empire was spelt out in more detail in an exchange of notes between Britain, France and Russia in 1916, referred to subsequently as the Sykes-Picot agreement. French and British spheres of influence were mapped out and Palestine was designated as an international sphere of influence. However, in 1917 the celebrated Balfour Declaration, issued by the British Foreign Secretary, promised a national home in Palestine for the Jewish people. In a further agreement, drawn up at St Jean de Maurienne in April 1917, Britain and France agreed to the establishment of an Italian sphere of influence in the region of Adalia and Smyrna. In July 1917 Greece entered the war on the allied side. It was clearly going to be difficult after the conclusion of the war to reconcile Italian ambitions with those of France and Greece in the Near East, or to adjudicate on the claims of Arabs and Jews in Palestine.

There were difficulties too concerning the Pacific and China. Germany had been in no position to defend her Pacific colonies or to maintain the territorial and economic rights in Shantung province on the Chinese mainland which she held as 'concessions'. Japan, which entered the war as an ally of Britain in August 1914, lost no time in seizing the German Pacific possessions north of the Equator. Subsequently, in a secret agreement of 1917, concluded at a moment when the British Admiralty was desperate for Japanese naval assistance in the Mediterranean, she received an assurance of British support for her claims to these ex-German possessions, while herself promising to back British or Dominion claims to the German colonies already captured by Imperial troops south of the Equator. Furthermore, by the Twenty-One Demands of 1915 Japan had forced a weak and divided China to grant her, amongst other things, extensive economic and political privileges in Manchuria and Inner Mongolia and the right to dispose of German concessions in Shantung as she wished. The British had pledged support of her Shantung claims in the agreement of 1917 mentioned above, and in that same year the United States Secretary of State, Lansing, had guardedly acknowledged that 'special relations' existed between Japan, Shantung, southern Manchuria and eastern Mongolia, by virtue of their contiguity. However, the ruling warlord coalition in Peking, which itself declared war on Germany in August 1917, asserted that the Twenty-One Demands had no legal force since they had been signed by the Chinese government under duress. The problems arising out of these various claims were to lead to bitter disputes at the Paris peace conference.

Russia and Germany

The seizure of power in Russia by the Bolsheviks in November 1917 created a number of further difficulties for the peace-makers. The establishment of an avowedly workers' state, Bolshevik appeals to the proletarian classes in other European countries to rise up and challenge the capitalist order in a similar way, and Bolshevik slogans such as Trotsky's 'no annexations and no indemnities' were bound to cause alarm and even panic amongst the leaders of industrialized countries. Superimposed upon traditional fears of Russian imperialist ambitions was a new concern that the Bolshevik doctrines could subvert the existing social and political order in capitalist countries, which had been severely shaken by the impact of the war. Thus the Bolsheviks forced on to the agenda at Paris questions much wider than those anticipated before November 1917. Clearly, whatever territorial settlement was arrived at after the war would not be endorsed by Bolshevik Russia, whose leaders made no secret of the fact that they were out to destroy world capitalism, the imperialism it allegedly spawned, and the territorial strongholds through which it operated.

At the same time, Bolshevik weakness in the face of German military might in eastern Europe helped to shape the map of Europe after 1919. In March 1918 Bolshevik leaders had no alternative but to accept the draconian terms which Germany imposed upon them in the Treaty of Brest-Litovsk. Not only did Moscow recognize the independence of Finland, the Ukraine and the Baltic states, but it also agreed to the redrawing of Russia's western frontier far to the east. As a result, large areas of Poland were freed from Russian rule, and the subsequent defeat of Germany and Austria-Hungary cleared the way for the reconstitution of an autonomous Polish state. The defeat of the Habsburgs also enabled the independent state of Czechoslovakia to be established. Other national and racial groupings clamoured for statehood, including Galicians, Ruthenians and Georgians. While the peace-makers pored over maps, the forces of the contending claimants to the western parts of the former Russian empire and of Habsburg territories battled it out in a series of direct military confrontations throughout 1919 and early 1920. The territorial arrangements which were eventually concluded owed as much to the outcome of these clashes as to the negotiations at Paris.

How was the perceived threat of Bolshevik Russia to the political and economic influence of western European nations to be met in the post-war years? Traditionally, the Habsburg dominions had stood as the west's bulwark against the danger of Russian expansion. In more recent times, as Habsburg power had waned, Berlin had come to replace Vienna. At the end of the war, however, neither was a feasible proposition. Germany, it is true, was far from the shattered hulk which she came to resemble in 1945. The end of hostilities had come about not as the result of a crushing allied victory in the field, but because it had become perfectly clear to Germany's military leaders that her allies were at breaking point and that the civilian effort necessary to sustain her armies could no longer be guaranteed. The High Command had consequently instructed the politicians to sue for peace on the best terms available. German troops, however, were still in occupation of parts of France, Belgium and the Baltic states, and began to return to their homeland only after the signing of the armistice. Germany remained a major political and economic unit in the heart of Europe. But there could be no question of casting her as Europe's barrier-fortress against the Russians. Public opinion, on the contrary, demanded that she should suffer, and suffer heavily, through reductions in her territorial, military and economic strength. As for the Habsburg empire, this had already ceased to exist as an entity by the time the peace conference met, and its reconstitution was unthinkable, not least because of the strength of nationalist sentiment in its component regions, and the powerful patronage such sentiment enjoyed at Paris. Since no other solution presented itself, the problem was to be left unresolved. The difficulties which bedevilled international relations in the inter-war years stemmed in great measure from this power vacuum in eastern Europe.

The impact of the United States

The entry into the war of the United States in 1917 was a mixed blessing for the western allies. Militarily, it more than compensated for the withdrawal of Russia, and convinced the Germans, after the failure of their 1918 spring offensive, that victory was no longer a possibility. Politically, however, it raised acute problems. President Wilson's views on the nature of the war and the shape of a peace settlement to follow differed radically from those of Britain and France. To Wilson, the outbreak of the war was tangible proof of the failure of traditional European diplomacy, based on balances of power, armed alliances and secret negotiations. What Wilson sought to construct was a more just and equitable system of international relations, based on clear principles of international law and centred on a universal association of nations working through agreed procedures to maintain world order. Wilson believed that the United States should take the lead in the creation of such a system, and should at the same time pursue a related goal, the extension of democracy throughout the world. He saw this as a moral commitment, entrusted to the American people and their leaders by the founding fathers, and already in 1916 he had proclaimed that the object of the war should be 'to make the world safe for democracy'. In that same year, his views were endorsed by American voters when, albeit by a narrow margin, he was re-elected president. In 1917, when unrestricted German submarine warfare and fears of subversion in Central America drew the United States into the conflict, he seized his chance to

9

use the great economic and naval strength built up by the United States during its years of neutrality to bring pressure upon Britain and France to follow the trail he had blazed. Territorial changes in Europe were of little concern to Wilson or the American people, who themselves faced no immediate military threat. America's entry into the war was portrayed as a crusade for a more just system of international relations, for the right of self-determination and for democracy, with the United States at the helm.

Wilson's peace aims were outlined in a number of speeches in 1917 and 1918, but the most succinct statement was contained in a carefully prepared address delivered to Congress on 8 January 1918, which is known as the 'Fourteen Points' speech because of the number of heads under which he itemized his peace programme. A summary of the contents of this speech is given in Appendix Two. Particularly important were the assertion that the national groupings within the Habsburg and Turkish empires should be given the opportunity of autonomous development, and the call for a general association of nations. In this speech, and his many others delivered in the course of 1918, Wilson sought to distance himself from his European allies and their traditional diplomatic dealings. (To this end, the United States entered the war not as an ally but as an Associated Power.) He also sought to reassure the weary civilian populations of Europe that the prize to be won by military victory would be a better world, and to win support in every quarter of the globe for his ideal of a peace based on principles of justice, equality and democracy. As he declared in ringing tones, 'peoples and provinces are not to be bartered about from sovereignty to sovereignty as if they were chattels and pawns in a game. . .'.

The British reaction to these pronouncements was somewhat muted. Balfour felt that the Fourteen Points were 'admirable but very abstract' and *The Times* that Wilson 'did not take into account certain hard realities of the situation'. The French concern was more with the successful prosecution of the war than with the details of a future settlement. Nevertheless, Wilson did achieve success in widening the scope of allied war aims. Initially limited to the restoration of Belgium and Serbia and the return of Alsace-Lorraine to France, by the closing stages of the war they had come to include self-determination for Czechs, Poles, and other subject peoples in eastern and south-eastern Europe, opening the straits to world shipping, and establishing the President's League of Nations.

When the Fourteen Points were first outlined, German newspapers were scathing, denouncing them as hypocritical, and aimed in reality at the achievement of 'Anglo-Saxon world hegemony'. As defeat loomed nearer, however, the German tune changed. Wilson's peace programme and general attitude appeared to promise some protection for Germany against punitive French and British demands. Accordingly, on 4 October 1918, the German government formally asked the President to take steps to bring about a ceasefire as a preliminary to the negotiation of peace terms on the basis of his address of 8 January and subsequent speeches. It was only at this point that Wilson sought the official support of the Entente governments for his peace programme. They were far from happy, Lloyd George objecting in particular to Point Two, which would rule out future naval blockades by Britain, and Clemenceau insisting that Germany's agreement to pay compensation 'for all the damage done to the civilian population of the Allies and their property by [her] aggression' be written in. The United States made it clear, however, that unless the allies toed the line, she would conclude a separate peace with Germany, and further objections were dropped. The Supreme War Council, which had co-ordinated the allied war effort, accordingly agreed to a peace settlement based on the Fourteen Points but taking account of the two specific reservations mentioned. They were somewhat reassured by Wilson's envoy, House, who told the allied leaders that the President 'had insisted on Germany accepting all his speeches, and from these you could establish almost any point that anyone wished against Germany'. On 5 November, Wilson informed the Germans of allied acceptance of his peace programme with the addition of the two reservations. He added that if they desired a suspension of hostilities on this basis, they should approach directly the allied military commanders in the field. On 9 November, the Kaiser, whose removal Wilson insisted upon as a precondition for the opening of the peace negotiations, abdicated. Just two days later, in Marshal Foch's railway carriage in the forest of Compiègne, the Germans signed an armistice agreement.

This armistice agreement was drawn up by allied and Amer-

11

ican military and naval commanders, and was therefore wholly unconnected with Wilson's peace programme on which the Germans had sued for peace. In practice, however, the armistice was bound to constitute an important element in later decision-making, and no leaders were more aware of this than the French. Having suffered German invasions in 1870 and 1914, they were determined to ensure the permanent weakening of their dangerous neighbour territorially, economically and militarily. Wilson's peace programme did not at first sight serve this purpose, but it might do so if linked with sufficiently stringent armistice terms. In fact, these were not as harsh as some, including American generals, wished. Fear that Germany might be provoked into fighting on, or that she might be left too weak to cope with Bolshevik-inspired uprisings, saw to that. Nevertheless, they were severe. German troops were immediately to withdraw beyond the Rhine; former German territory on the left bank was to be occupied; and a ten-mile-wide zone on the right bank, stretching from the Netherlands to the Swiss frontier, was to be neutralized. Allied and American garrisons were to be established at the three principal Rhine crossings and in thirty-mile-deep bridgeheads on the other side of the river. The Germans were also to be deprived of large quantities of war material, including all their submarines and much of their surface fleet, air force and transport. Finally, the blockade of Germany was to continue until peace terms had been settled and accepted.

Even before the armistice had been signed, however, Wilson's position at the forthcoming peace conference as the spokesman for American aims had been dealt a savage blow. In the mid-term elections, held on 5 November, his Republican opponents, who were strongly critical of his methods of conducting foreign policy and of the idealism of his peace programme, made sweeping gains which won them majorities in both Houses of Congress. Since any peace treaty to which the United States was a party would have to be submitted for detailed scrutiny to the Foreign Relations Committee of the Senate, now chaired by an uncompromisingly hostile Republican leader, Henry Cabot Lodge, and since it would then require approval by a two-thirds majority in the Senate, now Republican-controlled, the President's chances of gaining acceptance at home of any settlement he might negotiate on the basis of his 'Fourteen Points' were seriously imperilled. When Woodrow Wilson set sail for Europe in December – the first President of the United States to travel overseas during his term of office – both he and the European leaders with whom he would have to negotiate were well aware that he no longer spoke authoritatively for his country.

Making the peace

Organization

Peace delegates and large numbers of their expert advisers began to assemble in Paris from the beginning of January 1919, though the first official meetings did not take place until the 12th. The Supreme War Council had already agreed that Britain, France, Italy and the United States would play a leading part in the proceedings, and that Japan should also be recognized as a leading allied power with general interests. What had not been settled, however, was the relationship between these five leading powers and the twenty-seven lesser allies who had specific interests in one or other aspect of the overall settlement (see Appendix One). The French government urged that major issues should be thrashed out privately between the five leading powers at sessions of the Supreme War Council. The resulting agreements could then be presented to the smaller powers for endorsement. Wilson, however, while not objecting to informal conversations amongst the leading representatives, believed that the conference itself, through plenary sessions of all its delegates, should formally initiate discussions and take final decisions. Otherwise, he feared that a small number of leaders would take the crucial decisions behind closed doors in the kind of secret diplomatic dealings he had so strenuously denounced in his wartime speeches.

Wilson managed to ensure that, in the early stages of the conference, the smaller powers participated in a wide range of general discussions through meetings of all official delegates, and through commissions set up by those meetings to consider items such as the establishment of a League of Nations, war guilt, reparations, and international labour legislation. At the same time, two representatives of each of the five leading powers met as a Council of Ten to deal with pressing political and military problems, such as the renewal of the armistice with Germany and the provision of food supplies to eastern Europe.

However, as soon as the discussion switched to more contentious issues like the disposition of ex-German colonies and the territorial claims in Europe of allies such as Serbia, Greece, Czechoslovakia, Belgium and Denmark, the leading powers increasingly settled them by mutual negotiation and agreement, without reference to plenary sessions of the conference. They set up territorial commissions to examine the claims put forward by their smaller allies, and their own expert advisers played a major part in framing recommendations which were, in large part, incorporated into the final peace treaties themselves. Disputed points were referred back to the Council of Ten or its successor, the Council of Four. The Council of Four, consisting of the leaders of Britain, France, Italy and the United States, came into being in March, at the height of bitter disputes amongst the leading powers over the central peace terms. By this stage of the conference it was clear that only secret, face-to-face discussions between Lloyd George, Clemenceau, Wilson and Orlando could resolve the most contentious conflicts of interest. Consequently, the major issues of peace were hammered out in daily, private and frequently stormy sessions between the four leaders.

Many vivid pictures have been painted of the negotiations between these four men. Clemenceau has been depicted as the tenacious but cynical 'Tiger', subordinating all issues to his obsession with guaranteeing future French security. Wilson has been pictured in theological guise, arguing dogmatically for a peace based on principles of justice and self-determination. Lloyd George has been portrayed as a political chameleon, charting a tricky course between the opposing views of the other two men while at the same time safeguarding British interests. Orlando, who could speak no English and was therefore at a disadvantage in the discussions, joined in only when the talks turned to the problems of the Adriatic region. He stormed out of the negotiations when he was not promised all the territorial gains he sought for Italy. There is some truth in the many sketches painted of the Council of Four discussions, but the records show that the process of bargaining was complex, with attitudes by no means fixed. The easiest way to summarize the settlement finally reached is to examine the principal areas of

14

discussion and dispute and outline the compromise solutions put forward.

The League of Nations

At the insistence of President Wilson, this was the first issue dealt with at the peace conference. A commission was set up to draft a constitution for the new international organization, and agreement was reached by mid-February, largely because of a prior series of meetings between American and British legal experts who produced a jointly agreed set of articles on which discussions could be based. French attempts to fashion the League as a military alliance which could automatically be directed against potential aggressors failed completely. The British Empire representatives, Lord Robert Cecil and Jan Smuts, worked with Wilson to produce a League that would operate as a loose and flexible organization of member states, pledging themselves to follow a number of set procedures in dealing with international crises. Disputes between member states were to be referred to the League Council for examination and proposed settlement, and only if members took the law into their own hands were sanctions to come into play. To work towards the establishment of a more peaceful international order, member states agreed to disarm 'to the lowest point consistent with national safety' and to respect and preserve 'the territorial integrity and existing political independence of all Members of the League'. French representatives urged strongly that the League should be empowered to direct its members to adopt specified policies or provide set numbers of troops to deal with a crisis, but their views were not acceptable to the great majority of delegates on the commission. Thus the League of Nations was constituted to operate, not as a league of democracies, as Wilson had originally envisaged, or as a military alliance as the French desired, but as a loose 'association of nations' as the French translation implied. It was agreed that the ex-enemy states should not be able to join until they had given solid proof of their intention to abide by international agreements and carry out the peace terms. Even without them, however, there would be sufficiently wide-ranging conflicts of interest between the various member states to substantiate French fears that it would be difficult to reach common agreement and take concerted action on issues which would be seen very differently by the individual members. Promoting international co-operation through collaboration on international labour legislation or the control of disease and drugs and the white slave traffic might well result in substantial achievements for the general good of mankind. Securing international peace through voluntary political co-operation would prove much more difficult.

Wilson had to return to the United States in February to wind up the business of the outgoing Congress and sign its bills. While there, he was on the receiving end of mounting criticism directed at United States membership of the League and the obligations it would entail. There was also sharp comment about the possibility of League interference in the affairs of the American hemisphere, hitherto shielded by the operation of the Monroe Doctrine. On his return to Paris, Wilson successfully pressed for inclusion in the League Covenant of extra clauses, one re-affirming the validity of international engagements or 'regional understandings like the Monroe Doctrine', another specifying that member states could leave the League if they so wished after giving two years' notice, and a third stipulating that if disputes arose from domestic sources, they could not be considered by the League. He also secured agreement from his colleagues that the League Covenant should constitute the first twenty-six articles of each peace treaty. By these means he hoped to damp down Republican criticisms of the League and make it impossible for Senators to attack it without disavowing the entire peace settlement. Lloyd George, Clemenceau and their Italian and Japanese colleagues tried very hard to extract concessions from Wilson in return for their agreement to these extra points, and, while the President managed to avoid committing himself to the naval limitations Lloyd George was seeking on the current United States naval programme, his bargaining position on other issues to be decided was undoubtedly weakened. Working with the British representatives, he agreed to prevent the insertion into the Covenant of a clause endorsing the principle of the equality of nations and the just treatment of their nationals, for which the Japanese were pressing and to which the Australian delegates, in particular, were bitterly opposed. But he found it increasingly difficult to secure acceptance for his proposals on subsequent issues, partly because the determination of the allies to pursue their aims was strengthened by the growing evidence of American detachment from the European settlement.

Mandates

One of the first issues to be discussed by the Council of Ten at the end of January was the disposition of German colonies and non-Turkish provinces of the Ottoman empire. There was complete agreement that Germany's overseas colonies, which had been seized by British, French, Dominion and Japanese troops during the war, should not be returned to her. Wilson was fully persuaded that Germany had treated her colonial subjects harshly before the war, but he also believed that the wishes and well-being of the colonial inhabitants should be an important factor in the disposition of the colonies. He was opposed to their outright annexation by their military conquerors, and put forward a proposal whereby they would be administered as mandated areas by more politically and economically advanced nations who would help them to develop into modern states under the general supervision of the League of Nations. Lloyd George was not opposed to this proposal, which he described as 'virtually a codification of existing British practice', but he explained that South Africa, Australia and New Zealand were concerned for their security and therefore wished to annex, respectively, German South-west Africa, New Guinea and Samoa. Japan, as previously noted, had already secured British diplomatic support for the retention of the former German possessions north of the Equator which she had seized during the war.

Wilson was adamant that outright annexation was out of the question; it would have been totally opposed to the principle outlined in the fifth of his Fourteen Points. The colonies must be held in trust and administered under the aegis of the League of Nations. Smuts suggested a compromise formula to bridge the difference between Wilson and the Dominion and Japanese representatives. The character of the mandate, he argued, would vary according to the stage of development of a population, the economic conditions and the geographical situation of the territory. There should be three categories of mandate: 'A' mandates for the most advanced areas, such as the Arab provinces formerly ruled by Turkey (Syria, Mesopotamia and Palestine), 'B' mandates for German East Africa, Togoland and the Cameroons, and 'C' mandates for the rest. These last territories, owing to 'sparseness of population', 'small size', 'remoteness from the centre of civilization' or 'geographical contiguity to the territory of the mandatory power', could best be administered as 'integral portions' of the territory of the mandatory power. This was paring mandatory obligations to the bone, but still the crisis was not fully resolved. The Dominions and Japan wanted the mandatory states to be named forthwith, before they were prepared to accept Smuts's compromise formulation. Wilson, however, was desperate to avoid the impression that the spoils of war were being divided out before the League of Nations was even constituted. After a fierce confrontation between Wilson and Prime Minister Hughes of Australia, a compromise was reached whereby Smuts's scheme was accepted as a 'provisional decision' subject to reconsideration when the League constitution had been drafted. Mandates were not actually assigned until May, so Wilson got his way on this and on the establishment of the system itself. However, the terms on which the mandates were to be administered were very much a concession to the Dominions and to Japan.

Military and naval terms

Disputes also arose over the naval and military terms of the peace settlement. Lloyd George managed to avoid discussion of the contentious issue of 'freedom of the seas' by agreeing that the whole question should be looked at by the League of Nations once it was fully operational. The allied and associated powers had already agreed at the time of the signing of the armistice that the German navy should be interned in a neutral or allied harbour, and soon afterwards it was escorted to Rosyth in the Firth of Forth, and thence to Scapa Flow in the Orkneys, where it was to remain while the peace negotiations settled its fate. There was much discussion amongst British, American, French and Italian naval chiefs as to whether the ships should be sunk or distributed amongst the powers in some agreed ratio. The British view was that the navy should be sunk and they persuaded the United States to support this move, but the French and Italians were reluctant to lose such a golden opportunity to strengthen their own fleets by the addition of German ships. The Germans themselves finally resolved the issue by sinking the fleet on 21 June, when it had become clear that, whatever was decided, the ships would not be allowed to return to Germany. The Germans had already handed over substantial numbers of submarines to the British naval authorities, and it was decided that in future they should be forbidden to possess submarines or naval aircraft. Furthermore, they were to be limited to 6 battleships, 6 light cruisers, 12 destroyers and 12 torpedo boats, all strictly defined in terms of permitted tonnage. The entire navy was to have no more than 1500 officers and warrant officers, enlisted on a voluntary basis. Fortifications and harbour works at Heligoland were to be demolished, and the Kiel Canal was to be given the same status in international law as the Suez and Panama canals.

As with the navy, the army was also to be strictly limited and to be forbidden the use of tanks, military aircraft or heavy artillery. There was considerable discussion amongst the allied and associated powers about the basis on which the army should be recruited. The French were prepared to allow an army, based on annual conscription, of about 200,000 men. Lloyd George, however, maintaining that conscription was 'the tap root of militarism', was insistent that the army should be a volunteer army serving twelve-year contracts. Clemenceau was finally willing to concede this point, but only on condition that the size of the army be reduced to 100,000 since its quality and fighting capacity would obviously be considerably greater than that of an army of raw conscripts. Wilson's hopes for the future could be clearly discerned in the preamble to the military section of the treaty with Germany: Germany was to be disarmed 'in order to render possible the initiation of a general limitation of the armaments of all nations'. Allied commissions of control were set up to supervise the carrying out of the military, naval and air clauses, but it was left to the German authorities to co-operate voluntarily. As the 1920s wore on, allied commissioners repeatedly complained that Germany was not complying with the peace terms relating to German disarmament. The Germans themselves, however, not only refuted this allegation but countercharged that, since the allies were not disarming, Germany should be allowed to rearm. The absence of time limits for the duration of the disarmament clauses was undoubtedly a crucial omission; it reinforced the German case that the terms should be revised in the light of changed circumstances. Like the reparations clauses, the naval and military clauses caused considerable bitterness in Germany and there was to be widespread evasion and contravention of the terms.

Reparations

No single issue caused more acrimony at the peace talks than the question of reparation payments. In accepting a peace based on the Fourteen Points, including the French definition of the terms on which restoration should be made, the Germans agreed to pay compensation for damage caused by German aggression 'by land, by sea and from the air'. But how was the damage to be assessed, and was Germany to pay for all of it? If interpreted as including such government costs as war pensions and separation allowances paid during the war, Germany's total liability would double. Could she afford to pay? Claims of £30,000 million were being advanced as entirely reasonable, but how could Germany pay such sums when the war had crippled her economy? The French, who had taken out huge loans themselves to cover the costs of fighting, expected that German finance would cover the costs of restoration of invaded territories and repayment of war debts. A long period of stiff repayments, in gold or goods, would have the added advantage of keeping Germany financially and economically weak.

However, this was not in Britain's long-term interests. While the British public clamoured for Germany to be made to pay 'to the uttermost farthing', Treasury officials, especially the economist John Maynard Keynes, were pointing out to Lloyd George that Britain's post-war economic recovery was crucially dependent on a general revival of trade. This could only happen if the economies of the leading industrial nations were buoyant enough to enable them to purchase British manufactures on a large scale. Before 1914, Germany had been one of Britain's best customers, but a Germany heavily in debt to the allied powers would not be able to buy British goods in sufficient quantities. Lloyd George was in a further dilemma. If Germany was only to pay for direct war damage caused, Britain would receive a very small part of the total payment. If, however, he could persuade his colleagues to include war pensions and separation allowances, as he finally managed to do, Britain would get a larger sum of money, but the German liability would be vastly increased.

The United States tried to limit Germany's liability by basing it on her ability to pay rather than on the total amount of allied claims. In pursuit of this aim, their representative on the Reparations Commission, John Foster Dulles (to be US Secretary of State in the 1950s), proposed that a formula be adopted requiring Germany to admit a moral and theoretical responsibility for the entire cost of the war, while accepting an actual liability for only civilian damage. His formula was incorporated into the Treaty of Versailles as article 231, which became known as the 'war guilt' clause:

> The Allied and Associated Governments affirm and Germany accepts the responsibility of Germany and her allies for causing all the loss and damage to which the Allied and Associated Governments and their nationals have been subjected as a consequence of the war imposed upon them by the aggression of Germany and her allies.

This clause, more than any other in the entire Treaty of Versailles, was to cause lasting resentment in Germany, but ironically it was inserted in order to provide a clear basis on which reparations could be exacted, and to limit the overall sum. Germany was in fact to be liable only for 'civilian damage', except in the case of Belgium which was to receive from Germany her full war costs, because her invasion had been a violation of the treaties which in 1839 had guaranteed Belgian neutrality.

The Americans had their own reasons for endeavouring to limit German reparation payments. They were owed considerable sums of money by the allied powers, and the suggestion had already been floated by some British officials that the powers should consider an all-round cancellation of war debts and reparations. The repayment of war debts was likely to be financed out of German reparation payments, and therefore the United States worked to conclude a reparations settlement based on Germany's capacity to pay and yet substantial enough to satisfy the European allies. In the atmosphere of early 1919, this was asking the impossible. Clemenceau could not retreat from the astronomic sums the French public had been led to expect. In April, Lloyd George received a telegram signed by 376

Members of Parliament, much publicized in the popular press, urging him to 'present the bill in full' to the Germans. The consequence of all these conflicting pressures was that the exact total of reparations to be paid by Germany was not stated in the Treaty of Versailles. Instead, a Reparations Commission, comprising representatives of the leading allied and associated powers, plus Belgium, was established, to settle the figure after detailed consideration. The Germans angrily complained that they were being asked to sign a 'blank cheque'.

In fact, the delay in naming the sum worked to Germany's advantage. By the time the Reparations Commission seriously considered the question, it had become very clear that Germany would not be able to pay anything like the sums originally demanded by the French and by some British representatives at Paris. In 1921, Germany's liability to pay was established at £6000 million, and even this sum was progressively reduced and payments recycled to ease her burden. German nationalists made tremendous political capital out of the sums demanded, though the German nation succeeded in evading payment on anything but the most nominal level. At the same time, reparations wrangles and demands from the United States for repayment of war debts set the allied powers at each other's throats, and was one of the most important factors which drove them apart after 1919.

The question of punishment for war criminals proved even more intractable. Not all the allied representatives were happy to contemplate the judicial murder of crowned heads of state. The Japanese, conscious of the semi-divine status of their own Emperor, were particularly reluctant to sanction such a move. If the demands of the British and French publics to 'hang the Kaiser' were to be satisfied, he had first to be handed over to the allies. The Dutch government refused to yield him up, despite threats that Holland might not be allowed to join the League of Nations until it did. It proved equally difficult to draw up a list of lesser war criminals. Eventually, a handful of German military commanders and submarine captains were tried, not by the allies themselves, but by a German military court at Leipzig. The sentences imposed were light – fines or short terms of imprisonment – but this was the first time that the concept of 'crimes against humanity' was given legal sanction.

Negotiations about national frontiers were naturally extremely contentious. While expert commissions laboured to demarcate frontiers in eastern Europe to accord as far as possible with Wilson's insistence on 'self-determination of peoples', Clemenceau and Foch battled with Lloyd George and Wilson to weaken Germany in the west. The French demands for a Rhine frontier for Germany, the establishment of an independent Rhineland state and a Saar under French occupation almost brought the conference to a premature end in early April 1919, when Wilson ordered his ship to stand by to carry him back to the United States. Painfully, however, a series of compromises was reached.

Wilson had already accepted the French argument that, as partial compensation for the German destruction of coal mines and iron ore works in north-east France, the French government should be allowed unrestricted access to the coal mines of the Saar, which had produced 8 per cent of Germany's coal before the First World War. However, he was not prepared to agree to the further French demand that the Saar should be separated from Germany and placed under French sovereignty or allied control. The agreement finally reached was that the Saar should be administered by the League of Nations for fifteen years, with French ownership of the mines, and that after that time the inhabitants could choose in a plebiscite whether they wished to continue the existing arrangement, revert back to Germany or become a part of France.

The argument over the Saar was part of a larger argument over the whole Rhineland area. Neither Wilson nor Lloyd George was willing to concede the central French demand that the German frontier in the west should follow the course of the Rhine. Lloyd George saw only too clearly that this could sow the seeds for future conflict, just as the German annexation of Alsace and Lorraine in 1871 had been one of the long-term causes of the First World War. Clemenceau, however, pointed out that British security had been underwritten by the seizure of German colonies and restriction of the German navy. All France was seeking was equivalent security for her own territory. But Wilson and Lloyd George would not yield on the demand for a Rhine frontier for Germany. Instead, each leader offered the

French Prime Minister a treaty of guarantee of military assistance against unprovoked aggression, to operate under the League of Nations once it was fully established. While this served to resolve the deadlock, there were serious doubts amongst American and British delegates about whether the American Senate would ratify such a guarantee. Accordingly, when the British treaty of guarantee passed through Parliament in late spring it contained a clause to the effect that the treaty would not come into operation until the equivalent American treaty with France had been ratified.

Germany therefore retained possession of the Rhineland, but Wilson came to an agreement with Clemenceau that it should be occupied by allied troops for fifteen years, to ensure that the terms of the peace treaty were carried out. The area under occupation was to be divided into three zones, the most northerly to be evacuated after five years, the middle zone after ten years, and the most southerly after fifteen years, providing that Germany was meeting all her treaty obligations. Lloyd George was extremely reluctant to agree to an occupation of such length, because of the heavy costs in terms of money and manpower, but he was pressured into acceptance by his French and American colleagues. Germany herself was forbidden to keep military forces or military installations in the Rhineland, but no time limit was set on this restriction, and this again played into the hands of German nationalists in later years. As a further part of the territorial settlement in the west, Germany ceded Eupen and Malmédy to Belgium.

In eastern Europe, instead of quarrels over existing frontiers there were disputes about the establishment of the frontiers of the new states which were seeking recognition as the heirs to the lands of the former Russian and Habsburg empires. Given the mix of nationalities and races in this area, drawing frontiers along clearly defined national boundaries would be impossible. If strategic and economic considerations were given due weight, considerable minorities were bound to be created in all the east European states. The difficulties were clearly revealed in the demarcation of Poland's frontiers. Wilson's thirteenth point promised an independent Poland to include territories 'inhabited by indisputably Polish populations' which should be guaranteed 'free and secure access to the sea'. But this access to the sea would cut through the German provinces of Posen and West

Prussia, inhabited predominantly by German-speaking peoples. And if Poland obtained the port of Danzig, with its close-on half a million German inhabitants, about 2 million Germans would be included in the new Polish state. Largely on economic and strategic grounds, British and American experts agreed with their French counterparts that Danzig, and the provinces of Marienwerder and possibly Allenstein, should be assigned to Poland along with a substantial 'corridor'. Lloyd George, however, strongly disagreed, and largely because of his pressure Danzig was finally established as a Free City, to be administered by the League of Nations and to be connected with Poland by a customs union and port facilities. Poland would also control Danzig's foreign relations. Lloyd George also secured plebiscites for the inhabitants of Allenstein and Marienwerder through which they could indicate their preference for inclusion in Germany or Poland. The plebiscites were duly held in March 1920, and both districts voted decisively for inclusion in Germany.

Upper Silesia was another racially mixed area on the German-Polish frontier, of immense economic value. Before the war, it had provided Germany with 23 per cent of her coal, 80 per cent of her zinc and a large part of her iron. The Polish territorial commission assigned it to Poland on the grounds that it was 'indisputably Polish in origin'. Only after violent German objections in late May did Lloyd George press for a change of heart and, at the very least, for a plebiscite to be held. Again he was successful, and the plebiscite was eventually held in 1921 to determine the fate of the region. In this case, however, the populations were so inextricably mixed that it was extremely difficult to fix a frontier along lines of nationality. In the end, a special League of Nations commission divided Upper Silesia between Germany and Poland, with the western, predominantly agricultural, section going to Germany, and the smaller but wealthier eastern section being assigned to Poland.

Fixing the frontiers elsewhere in the east proved just as awkward, especially in the absence of Russian representation at Paris. With Bolshevik attention concentrated on internal security, German abrogation of the Treaty of Brest-Litovsk (see p. 8), enabled Finland, Estonia, Latvia and Lithuania to be established as independent states. Czechoslovak and Romanian territorial claims were treated generously at the expense of Austria and Hungary, but outstanding territorial disputes remained unresolved, especially between Poland and Lithuania over Vilna, and between Poland and Czechoslovakia over Teschen. In the circumstances it can be argued that the treaties went as far as they could to reflect the claims of nationality and self-determination, taking into account strategic and economic considerations. The new states were required to sign minority treaties, to be administered under the watchful eye of the League, guaranteeing specified freedoms and rights to their minority subjects. Nevertheless, considerable friction was bound to remain between the different races, and nowhere were feelings stronger than amongst the large concentrations of Germans in Poland and Czechoslovakia. However well-treated they might be in the future, they were likely to be a source of dissatisfaction, liable to undermine stability in the new states. Successive German governments in the 1920s and early 1930s made it clear that they did not accept as permanent the territorial settlement in eastern Europe and wished to revise it. Added aggravation came with the stipulation that Germany was to respect the independence of Austria. German nationalists could argue in the future that rights of self-determination allowed to other races in eastern Europe were being denied to Germans.

Frontiers in the Adriatic and Mediterranean region

Principles of self-determination and nationality also caused problems in this area. Italy had come into the war after securing promises from Britain and France that victory would give her the Trentino, south Tyrol, Istria and part of Dalmatia. Wilson was not a party to the secret Treaty of London and was initially horrified by its terms, since they so clearly breached his ninth point, that Italy's frontiers should be adjusted along 'clearly recognizable lines of nationality'. However, by the time the conference started, he was persuaded to accept an Italian frontier stretching as far north as the Brenner pass. But difficulties now arose over Italy's north-eastern frontier with Serbia. Because of the complete collapse of Habsburg power, it was possible to construct a sizeable Serbo-Croat-Slovene state, which was to be called Yugoslavia after 1929. The Italians regarded this development, along with the establishment of an independent Albania, as potentially menacing to their security in the Adriatic. They demanded the inclusion of Fiume in Italy, in addition to Trieste which had already been promised. Fiume had been assigned, under the Treaty of London, to Croatia, and Croatia was to be absorbed into the new Serbo-Croat-Slovene state. The port of Fiume was the only possible economic outlet to the Adriatic for the new state, and neither Britain and France nor the United States was prepared to allow Italy to annex it. They suggested that it should be administered under the League, like the Saar and Danzig, but this was not acceptable to the Italian delegates who stormed out of the negotiations in late April. Great national passions were aroused in Italy, and no Italian leader could be seen to retreat on the issue. In September, troops under the leadership of a fervently nationalist Italian poet, D'Annunzio, seized Fiume for Italy. Negotiations about its final status dragged on for a year between the Italians, the allied powers and the Serbo-Croats, before agreement was eventually reached that it should become a Free City. Italian government troops accordingly drove out D'Annunzio and his nationalists, but showed no disposition to leave themselves. After Mussolini's seizure of power in Italy in late 1922, the new Yugoslav state was forced to accept that Fiume would remain in Italian possession.

It was not only in Italy that the stirring of deep national passions prevented the acceptance of peace terms. The peace negotiations with the Sultan of Turkey resulted in a treaty extremely favourable to the allies. The Straits of Constantinople were to remain open in peace and in war to merchant and war ships of all nations and were to be placed under the control of an international commission. Turkey renounced all rights in the Sudan and Libya, and recognized the French protectorates in Morocco and Tunis, the British protectorate in Egypt and British annexation of Cyprus. The Hedjaz (Saudi Arabia) was to become independent, and Syria, Mesopotamia and Palestine were to be helped towards independence by Britain and France acting as 'A' category mandatory powers. The Greeks were to continue their occupation of Smyrna and would receive some Turkish Aegean islands and eastern Thrace. Kurdistan was to become autonomous and Armenia was to become an independent state.

These terms were embodied in the Treaty of Sèvres, signed in 1920 by the Sultan after the allied military occupation of Constantinople but never ratified. A nationalist revolt, under the leadership of Mustapha Kemal, challenged the predominance of the allies and the humiliating submission of the Sultan. Two years of fighting ensued, and in 1923, after the deposition of the Sultan and a string of rousing military successes, in the course of which the Turks drove the Greeks out of Smyrna, a new treaty was negotiated with the allies at Lausanne. This was far more favourable to Turkey, which now regained Smyrna, eastern Thrace, part of Armenia and some of the Aegean islands, though the Straits were to remain demilitarized.

The Far East

In the Far East, as we have seen, Japan had built up for herself a strong position. Not only had she seized the Pacific Caroline and Marianne islands north of the Equator, but she had also occupied the harbour of Kiaochow, leased by the Chinese to Germany in the 1890s, and then the entire province of Shantung. At Paris, the Chinese delegates demanded that the German concessions in the province, and the port of Kiaochow, should be returned to China. Japan argued that Germany had yielded them up to her, and that she would negotiate about them not at the conference itself but in direct talks with the Chinese. Already in 1918, in an exchange of notes with the Chinese warlord government in Peking, the Japanese had laid claim to rights far in excess of those the Germans had enjoyed. They had also secured the agreement of the United States that 'territorial contiguity' assured Japan of a special position on the Chinese mainland, and her claims had received diplomatic backing from Britain and France during the war. Wilson was therefore unable to pressurize the Japanese representatives at Paris into giving up their country's occupation of Kiaochow and Shantung. He was forced to recognize the existing position, rationalizing the agreed settlement to his press secretary as 'the best that could be had out of a dirty past'. Acceptance of the situation, however, aroused great nationalist demonstrations in China, orchestrated by students in Peking. The Chinese delegates refused to sign the Treaty of Versailles, and this reinforced growing disquiet over the agreement in the United States. Criticism of the Shantung settlement was one of the major factors leading to the United States' failure to ratify the Treaty of Versailles. Eventually, in 1922, as part of the Washington Treaty agreements, Japan agreed to return the port and province to China, retaining only the economic concessions.

28

The Treaty of Versailles was completed in great haste at the end of April, and handed to German representatives at Versailles on 7 May. Few of its 440 clauses had not been the subject of intense bargaining and serious disagreement, and while it had been the original intention to invite enemy delegates to join the conference when a preliminary peace settlement had been drawn up, the difficulties of reaching a settlement at all made this impossible. The Germans were given fifteen days, later extended by a week, to comment on the treaty, and this they did at great length. Their bitter and sustained objections, documented in great detail, were received by the allied and associated powers at the end of May. They reinforced growing feelings, particularly amongst the British representatives, that the treaty as a whole was too harsh. Some, like Nicolson and Keynes, criticized it because it departed so radically from Wilson's Fourteen Points. Others, like Lloyd George and Smuts, felt that though the individual clauses were reasonable, the overall effect was sufficiently punitive for the Germans to refuse to sign it. There was therefore an eleventh-hour attempt by the British delegation to press for modifications in response to the German objections. As already mentioned, the demand for a plebiscite in Upper Silesia was accepted. Less successful were British demands for a much shorter military occupation of the Rhineland, the immediate admission of Germany into the League of Nations, and the reconsideration of the reparations settlement. Wilson in particular took a strong stand against making changes at this late stage for reasons of political expediency. Consequently the treaty, which the Germans finally signed on 28 June 1919 in the same Hall of Mirrors at Versailles in which the French had been forced to acknowledge their submission after the Franco-Prussian war in 1871, was only a slight modification of the original version.

The signing of the Treaty of St Germaine-en-Laye with Austria followed on 10 September, and that of the Treaty of Neuilly with Bulgaria on 27 November. The Treaty of Trianon with Hungary was not signed until 4 June 1920. While Bulgarian territorial losses were not great, the new state of Austria contained only a quarter of the area of the old, with only a fifth of the population – mainly concentrated in the capital, Vienna.

She was to be limited to a volunteer army of 30,000 men and to three police boats on the Danube. Hungary ceded to Romania more territory than she kept, and 3 million Magyars were placed under foreign rule.

Yet the main criticisms against the unjustness of the treaties came from Germany. Attempts to carry out the military and reparations sections aroused storms of protest from nationalist groups, and charges of betrayal of the Fatherland. Yet the Treaty of Versailles was not excessively harsh on Germany, either territorially or economically. It deprived her of about 13½ per cent of her territory (including Alsace Lorraine), about 13 per cent of her economic productivity and about 7 million of her inhabitants – just over 10 per cent of her population – as well as her colonies and large merchant vessels. However, the German people were expecting victory and not defeat. It was the acknowledgement of defeat, as much as the treaty terms themselves, which they found so hard to accept.

For the victors, the treaty represented an uneasy compromise between Wilsonian idealism, French security requirements and British pragmatism. Wilson looked to the League to remove its worst blemishes, Clemenceau sought to carry it out to the letter, and Lloyd George was under strong domestic pressure from June 1919 onwards to revise it. Even before the treaty was ratified in January 1920, Keynes had written a devastating critique of the way the treaty had been negotiated, drawing attention in particular to the unworkability and undesirability of the reparations clauses. The publication of Keynes's *Economic Consequences of the Peace* in December 1919 fed growing hostility towards the treaty in the United States, and both in November 1919 and in March 1920 the United States Senate failed to ratify the Treaty of Versailles by the necessary two-thirds majority. Wilson himself suffered a serious stroke in the autumn of 1919, but from his sickbed he urged his supporters not to compromise with the Republicans on a list of reservations to the treaty which they were drawing up, and to vote for the treaty alone. Wilson's supporters, voting against the treaty because of the attached list of reservations, joined together with extreme Republicans opposed to the whole treaty to deny it the two-thirds majority. Thus within a year of the peace conference, the victorious alliance which had defeated Germany and negotiated a set of peace terms had crumbled away. It was this critical collapse, rather than the provisions of the peace terms themselves, which ensured that the Treaty of Versailles was never fully accepted or enforced. Negotiations at the peace conference exposed the divisions between the victorious powers and opened the rifts. Attitudes towards enforcement and revision of the peace terms widened them into a great chasm which fatally divided the powers seeking to uphold the peace settlement.

Keeping the peace

The enforcement of a peace settlement negotiated with such great difficulty required the same determination and co-operation amongst the victorious powers as the winning of the war. No leader was more aware of this than Clemenceau who, on the day of the signing of the armistice in 1918, had commented: 'we have won the war: now we have to win the peace, and it may be more difficult'. The European allies had not been able to defeat Germany and the other Central Powers without the help of the United States. The peace settlement itself assumed the form it did largely because of American participation in peace-making. Five months after protesting German delegates signed the Treaty of Versailles, the United States withdrew its political support and this change of policy was confirmed in March 1920. The United States signed a separate peace treaty with Germany, and did not become a member of the League of Nations. The treaty of guarantee, offered to France in March 1919 as an alternative to a Rhine frontier, was never considered by the Foreign Relations Committee of the Senate. Consequently, the British government decided not to proceed further with its own treaty of guarantee to France.

The worst fears of French leaders were now realized. France's pre-war ally, Russia, no longer had a common frontier with Germany and was in the throes of civil war. If the Bolshevik regime survived, it was not likely to want to work with France to contain possible German expansion. Her wartime ally, Britain, was unwilling to guarantee military assistance in the event of unprovoked attack, and her late associate, the United States, was in the process of detaching herself completely from the political affairs of Europe. France, with her population dwindling below 40 million, was to be left alone to face her German

31

neighbour, who had a population approaching 70 million, and who still retained considerable economic and industrial strength which could provide the basis for future military aggression.

In this situation, France's response was to insist upon the most stringent enforcement of the peace terms and to conclude military agreements with Poland and Czechoslovakia aimed at the encirclement of Germany. With a post war army of some 600,000 men and a strong airforce, she refused to contemplate any measures of disarmament until the British government was prepared to offer some tangible guarantees of military assistance.

Without the prospect of United States support, however, the British government was reluctant to underwrite French security. At the same time, aggressive post-war moves by the United States to build up its navy and to pursue with vigour its trading interests in South America and the Far East posed serious problems for Britain. Both Britain and France were on the retreat as world powers and striving to hold on to their overseas possessions in increasingly turbulent times. France faced nationalist challenges in her North African territories, in Indo-China and in her newly acquired mandatory charge, Syria. A post-war British army of 300,000 had to cope with troubles in Ireland and growing nationalism in Egypt and India. Peace-keeping in Palestine and Mesopotamia was a further drain on manpower and resources. Britain's Dominions were making increasing demands on her: Canada and South Africa for more independence, and Australia and New Zealand for a greater say in decision-making. Both Britain and France had sold off overseas investments during the war, and were clinging desperately to overseas markets in an increasingly competitive world.

Clearly, Britain's pre-war position as the world's leading naval and trading power was under threat. Strong voices called for British governments to devote their efforts to the development of empire and the strengthening of Britain's position overseas. A strict enforcement of the territorial settlement in Europe, necessitating armies of occupation, commissions of control in the Rhineland and treaties of military guarantee to France, would reduce Britain's capacity to maintain a strong presence outside Europe, by increasing expenditure and diverting manpower. What was needed in Europe was as rapid a return as possible to pre-war political and economic stability, boosting Britain's trade prospects and freeing her from expensive political and military involvement. The means to this end was seen to lie not through strict enforcement of the treaty but through German acceptance of the main bulk of its terms. British political leaders argued that this could be secured only after detailed discussion and revision of the more contentious terms, in direct negotiations with German representatives. They tried to persuade their French colleagues to co-operate in this process, and to adopt policies which would appease Germany and ensure her co-operation in the achievement of stability in Europe.

But post-war French leaders did not see the appeasement of Germany as a step on the road to the restoration of peace and stability in Europe. They feared that treaty revision would inevitably strengthen Germany and lead to her economic and military domination of Europe, resulting in a German war of revenge, with the invasion and defeat of France as its prime objective. Such an outcome could be avoided only by a policy of strict treaty enforcement, backed up if possible by a firm Anglo-American military pact. Successive British governments, however, were reluctant either to endorse strict treaty enforcement or to enter into military agreements with France, and this reluctance inevitably reinforced French fears for the future and unwillingness to pursue conciliatory policies or schemes involving disarmament. Britain and France were thus in total disagreement on the means through which lasting peace in Europe could be achieved, and on their policies towards Germany. The result was a series of conflicts between the two powers in their policies towards eastern and south-eastern Europe, over the key issues of reparations, disarmament and security, and over the role and activities of the League of Nations.

Eastern and South-Eastern Europe

United States withdrawal from political involvement in post-war Europe made it extremely difficult for the allied powers to stabilize the situation in this part of Europe. It had already been apparent during the peace negotiations that the leading powers were unable to exert a decisive influence over the activities and ambitions of the new east European states, and beyond them raged a civil war in Russia. Allied intervention failed to overthrow the Bolshevik government, and allied military occupation

33

of Constantinople provoked a nationalist uprising in Turkey which challenged the newly established territorial settlement in the whole of the Near East. Polish nationalist ambitions spilled over into military confrontations with Galicians, Lithuanians and Bolsheviks. In 1920, Polish forces advanced on Kiev in the Ukraine before being pushed back by Bolshevik troops almost to the gates of Warsaw. The frontier between Russia and Poland was not clearly demarcated until 1921 when, by the Treaty of Riga, some 3 million Russians were assigned to Polish rule. The line of demarcation could hardly be regarded as stable or secure by either side, and the Poles could not feel other than vulnerable to future territorial challenge from either Russia or Germany.

The new east European states were racially mixed amalgams of territories at very different stages of economic development, and the process of national unification was bound to be long and painful. The attempt to establish democratic institutions and procedures in these new states, and the adoption of policies of far-reaching land reform, made the attainment of political and economic stability even more difficult. Each newly constituted state was looking to safeguard and strengthen its own political base and economic development, and the consequence was the fragmentation of eastern Europe not just politically but economically. United States finance and credit could have made a major contribution to the stabilization of eastern and south-eastern Europe. In its absence, the social and economic tensions within the new states kept them weak and sapped the foundations of the territorial settlement, leaving it open to challenge in the 1930s.

The economies of the east European states were further strained by the considerable armies which were built up, especially by the 'Little Entente' powers of Yugoslavia, Czechoslovakia and Romania, and by Poland. The 'Little Entente' powers had a common interest in protecting their considerable territorial gains against the possibility of a resurgent Hungary. To this end, they worked together diplomatically and militarily. Poland, sandwiched between Germany and Russia, built up an army of a quarter of a million men to protect her newly established frontiers against future aggression from east or west. But her future security did not lie in her own military strength so much as in the diplomatic and military ambitions of her mighty neighbours. Both Poland and her neighbour Czechoslovakia owed their existence to the military defeat of Germany and Austria-Hungary and the collapse of Tsarist Russia. They both contained large concentrations of German-speaking inhabitants. Any agreement between Britain, France and Germany on treaty revision involving territorial changes in eastern Europe was likely to affect them adversely, and any increase in German economic or military strength could pose a serious threat to their very existence. Not surprisingly, therefore, these two east European states worked closely with France to ensure that, while the peace treaties were strictly observed, particularly in relation to the disarmament of Germany, they could together mobilize armies totalling well over a million men.

However, the repudiation by the United States of the entire peace settlement increased the reluctance of successive British governments in the 1920s to underwrite in any tangible way this part of the European territorial settlement. It was in eastern Europe that Lloyd George had secured his greatest success in revising the peace terms in Germany's favour. Many political leaders in inter-war Britain shared with him a belief that the new states of eastern Europe were unreliable and inherently unstable. They might fall under Bolshevik influence, and they could not, for many years, provide the political stability and orderly administration to which their German-speaking minorities had been accustomed as former members of the German and Habsburg empires. It seemed obvious that future German governments would press for territorial modifications in the east, starting with the desire to link East Prussia more closely with the rest of Germany, and no British government was prepared after 1919 to close the door to that possibility. Therefore, successive British governments took care to confine any specific political or military commitments they might make to western Europe, although under article 10 of the League Covenant they had undertaken to 'preserve . . . against external aggression the territorial integrity and existing political independence of all members of the League'. They hoped to persuade France and her eastern allies to agree to peaceful territorial revision of the frontiers in eastern Europe in negotiations between Germany and her neighbours. But such agreement was not forthcoming in the 1920s, and many British politicians therefore had some sympathy with Nazi German leaders who argued, in the 1930s, that they were forced to seek territorial

35

revision in the east by force, because peaceful revision through negotiated agreements had been blocked by the refusal of France and her eastern allies to enter into any discussions on the subject.

British and French differences of attitude and policy in eastern Europe were repeated in the Near East. Britain backed the Greeks against the challenge from Mustapha Kemal's Turkish troops, while France came to a secret accommodation with the new nationalist regime at Ankara. When the Turkish forces drove the Greeks out of Smyrna in 1922, British troops at Chanak, on the other side of the Straits, stood alone to face the Turkish onslaught. A military confrontation was avoided, largely due to the cool judgement of British military and naval commanders on the spot, but Anglo-French disunity could not have been more clearly revealed. It was the same story in the Middle and Far East – each government accusing the other of intrigue and secret dealings prejudicial to its own influence. The establishment of a Fascist regime in Italy in late 1922 added to the difficulties facing the two governments. For France, it raised the frightening prospect of two potentially aggressive neighbours who might in the future decide to work together. French political leaders accordingly aimed to appease Mussolini, in the hope that he would be prepared to act with them to keep Germany weak. If appeasement of Italy entailed the encouragement of her naval and colonial ambitions in the Mediterranean area, however, the British government would be bound to view this with concern, given the importance of the Mediterranean Sea as a vital link in the British Empire's world-wide chain of communications. The increasingly aggressive policies pursued by Italy and later in the 1920s by Japan posed a threat to the peace settlement which the British and French governments found considerable difficulty in countering, and added to the divisions of policy which were already apparent between them.

Reparations and disarmament

Between January 1920 and December 1922, twenty-three summit conferences were held between French, British, Italian and Belgian representatives. They followed a similar and predictable pattern. British representatives urged their French colleagues to relax the provisions of the Treaty of Versailles, especially the reparations and disarmament clauses. The French consented to minor concessions, but only on condition that, if Germany defaulted on the agreed reparations or disarmament terms, Britain would support allied occupation of German territory to secure German compliance. On two occasions, in 1920 and 1921, the result was a French occupation of German towns in the Ruhr, which Britain endorsed with the utmost reluctance. In April 1921, the Reparations Commission set Germany's total liability at £6000 million, but the German government remained extremely reluctant to pay. At the same time, members of the allied commissions of control, which were established to supervise the carrying out by Germany of the disarmament provisions of the Treaty of Versailles, reported numerous infringements and extreme disinclination on the part of the German authorities to co-operate with the commissioners or enforce compliance with the treaty terms.

French fears about Germany's long-term intentions were intensified during the Genoa conference, held in March 1922 to discuss issues of European disarmament and economic rehabilitation. The German and Russian delegates slipped away to nearby Rapallo and concluded a secret treaty. News of their rendezvous spread quickly amongst the conference delegates, and was bound to engender suspicion and anxiety, particularly amongst those from eastern Europe. From this time onwards, rumours circulated about secret Russo-German collaboration to evade the terms of the peace treaties. Newspapers carried reports about the illegal German manufacture and testing of tanks and military aircraft on Russian soil, and about German loans to build up Russia's armed strength. The possibility that Germany could collaborate closely with the Bolshevik regime in a challenge to the territorial settlement in Europe reinforced the determination of the British government to try to work with Germany for revision of the peace treaties, in order to wean her away from the malevolent influence of Russia. But the prospect of close Russo-German collaboration intensified feelings of insecurity in France and made her leaders more desperate to weaken Germany by any means possible.

In December 1922, the Reparations Commission declared Germany to be in default on deliveries of timber, though the British representative on the commission described the amount due as 'almost microscopic'. Once more a military show of force

37

was considered appropriate by France and Belgium to extract the reparations, and in January 1923 the Ruhr industrial area was invaded and occupied by French and Belgian troops. The French not only hoped to be able to collect the reparations at gunpoint but also wanted to try to fan the flames of Rhineland separatism, to see if there was any possibility of working towards the achievement of an independent Rhineland. Neither of these goals was achieved. Instead of a rising tide of support for Rhineland independence, the military invasion stirred up intense feelings of German nationalist hostility against France, which was increased by the appearance, within French units, of coloured troops. Instead of handing over reparations in kind, the German authorities in the Ruhr co-ordinated a campaign of passive resistance, and industrial production ground to a halt. The German mark, continually under pressure since 1919, began to depreciate rapidly against the dollar. The German government responded to the crisis by printing paper money, and by November 1923 the mark had slumped in value so dramatically that one dollar fetched 630 billion marks. Wages and salaries had to be revised daily along with prices, and a wheelbarrow piled high with notes was required to buy a loaf of bread. Hard-working, conscientious German families saw their life savings wiped out overnight, while those with debts and large overdrafts, or with access to foreign currency, profited handsomely from the crisis.

The invasion of the Ruhr in 1923 had the most serious consequences. Within Germany, it weakened the position of the middle classes in society, and diminished their support for the Weimar government. Extremist parties on the right and the left were given a boost, because of the alarm at the prospect of complete economic collapse and social disorder. Many historians argue that the invasion of the Ruhr paved the way for Hitler's subsequent rise to power. Both the British government and the British public were alienated by French policies so obviously designed to dismember and cripple Germany. The French franc itself came under pressure and the French government learned painfully that direct action carried a high political and economic cost. Henceforth the French government worked to contain Germany in the west, not by offensive action but by defensive measures, in particular by the construction of the Maginot line. It has been suggested that France's failure to take military action to stop Hitler's remilitarization of the Rhineland in 1936 stemmed largely from the unhappy experience in the Ruhr in 1923.

The crisis was resolved only by the intervention of the United States which, alarmed by its effect on the international money markets, despatched General Dawes to Europe to work with the Reparations Commission and with economic experts to find a solution to the reparations tangle. The resulting Dawes settlement, agreed in 1924, included a two-year moratorium on reparations payments, the end of the military occupation of the Ruhr, and the raising of a £40 million loan for Germany. A schedule of future reparations payments was established, and the German government promised to meet it. Thus began the celebrated triangular flow of money between the United States and Europe. American loans enabled Germany to pay reparations to France and Britain; the French and British governments negotiated debt-funding settlements with the United States Treasury, and began the repayment to America of their war debts. American loans also enabled the Germans to build new factories, houses and schools, while making only minimum reparations payments. Meanwhile, European stocks of gold drained away into American vaults, making those European currencies which were backed by gold increasingly vulnerable. Yet despite the loans, Germany protested that payment was causing economic hardship and, in 1929, a new reparations schedule was drawn up with the help of the American economic expert Owen Young. A new loan of £60 million was promised to Germany, and a revised scale of reparations, spread over fifty-nine years, agreed upon. As part of this package, Britain and France agreed to terminate their occupation of the Rhineland, five years ahead of schedule. However, the onset of the Depression in 1929 rendered the Young settlement abortive. In 1932, a moratorium on reparations payments was agreed, and only token war debts payments exchanged hands after that date.

The whole issue of reparations and war debts showed clearly that, while the United States might turn its back on Europe politically, it could not dissociate itself economically, since it was now the dominant power in international finance, inextricably linked to the other leading industrial nations of the world. The refusal of successive administrations to help their wartime associates in the task of repairing and restoring the economic fabric of

Europe by the granting of credits contributed significantly to the failure to establish in Europe a lasting peace. The strict policy of separating war debts from reparation payments, and insisting on full and early repayment of the former, was a short-sighted policy not at all conducive to American long-term economic interests. As a trading nation, the United States was working to build up world trade and prosperity, and this could only be achieved by two-way flows of goods, money and credit. In the 1920s the flow was heavily one-way, and the result was an economically depressed and politically fragile Europe. It was a mistake the United States did not repeat after the Second World War.

Achievements in the field of disarmament were also disappointing. The allies had disarmed Germany as a first step in the process of general European and world disarmament. We have already seen how difficult it was to enforce measures of disarmament on an unwilling German government. To persuade other powers to follow suit was an even more difficult task. Naval disarmament proved easier to promote than the limitation of armies. In 1922, at Washington, the United States, Britain, Japan, France and Italy agreed to the limitation of their capital ship strength in a fixed ratio. To some extent, this agreement was made possible by the growing realization that the massive capital ship was being gradually rendered obsolete by new developments in military and naval technology. Significantly, it did not prove possible to reach agreement on the abolition of submarines, or to set limits to the numbers of cruisers and destroyers. At the same time, under American pressure, Britain also terminated her alliance with Japan, and it was replaced by a four-power pact between the United States, Britain, Japan and France. Japan agreed to restore Shantung to Chinese control, with the exception of certain economic concessions, and nine powers with trading interests in China agreed to respect Chinese integrity and to promote equal economic opportunities in their Chinese spheres of influence.

In 1927, an attempt was made at Geneva to extend the agreement reached on capital ships to cruisers, but no basis for limitation could be reached, either between the United States and Britain or between France and Italy. In 1930, at a conference in London, the United States, Britain and Japan finally agreed to limit their cruisers in a fixed ratio, but it became clear as the negotiations proceeded that the Japanese naval authorities were becoming increasingly restless at Anglo-American attempts to limit Japanese naval strength. By the terms of the treaty of Washington, Britain and America had agreed not to fortify military bases within a certain radius of Japan, thereby making it extremely difficult for either power to carry out a policy of naval or military containment of Japan. Only carefully co-ordinated, joint American and British action could check Japanese expansion outside her stipulated zones of influence in the Pacific, and acrimony over war debts, naval disarmament proposals and conflicts of economic interest in the Far East made such co-operation difficult to envisage. When Japan invaded Manchuria in September 1931, no co-ordinated countermeasures on the part of America and Britain were forthcoming, and some historians have argued that Japan's unchecked seizure of Manchuria encouraged nationalist leaders in Europe to pursue their aggressive ambitions with more vigour and less fear of military retaliation.

If naval limitation schemes met with mixed success, attempts to draw up a draft arms limitation convention agreeable to the major world powers and to members of the League failed completely. At Geneva, a preparatory disarmament commission met from 1926 and took five years to compile an agreement which could be discussed by government representatives. The scheme was examined in detail in sessions of a Disarmament Conference, organized by the League of Nations, which met from 1932 to 1934, but agreement could not be reached on ways of assessing fighting capacity or on the basis on which armies should be limited. In view of the failure of other powers to implement measures of arms limitation, German representatives demanded the right to rearm, and made it clear in the course of 1933 that if this right was not secured through negotiation, the German government was prepared to flout the provisions of the Treaty of Versailles and take action to build up her armed forces. Germany subsequently withdrew from the Disarmament Conference and gave notice of her intention to leave the League. Again, there was some sympathy for her case in Britain. France and her eastern allies had consistently refused to reduce their armed strength, while Germany had been restricted to an army of 100,000 men. It did not seem reasonable to expect German governments to accept this restriction on a permanent basis, and yet all attempts to negotiate revision had failed. It was only natural, argued many politicians in Britain, that the German government would want to take action in due course to build up her armed forces, or face a challenge from opposition parties urging more positive action. Once again, therefore, Anglo-French disagreement enabled Germany to seize the initiative, and with Hitler now at the helm the consequences were menacing for European peace.

Security

The main reason put forward by France and her eastern allies for their failure to disarm was that they felt insecure, and that until they could be assured of military support in the face of unprovoked aggression they could not contemplate any measures of arms limitation. In 1919, France had sought guarantees of military assistance from the United States and Britain, but these had not materialized. From 1920 to 1925, French leaders endeavoured to pressurize the British government into agreeing to an alliance which would include a promise of British military help. Lloyd George and Briand agreed on a draft treaty between their two countries at Cannes in January 1922, but its terms were not specific on the precise nature of the military assistance Britain was prepared to offer. When French leaders pressed for more binding military agreements, talks were broken off. In March 1925, the British Foreign Secretary, Austen Chamberlain, proposed to the British Cabinet that Britain should conclude an alliance with France, but his suggestion was turned down. Thus, French efforts to secure an alliance with Britain in the early 1920s failed, and contributed to France's refusal to contemplate serious measures of treaty revision or disarmament.

Having failed to achieve security through the conclusion of an alliance with Britain, France attempted to strengthen the machinery of the League of Nations so that it would be empowered to take rapid military action to deal with unprovoked aggression. But again Britain blocked French moves by rejecting both the Draft Treaty of Mutual Assistance in summer 1924, and the Geneva Protocol in 1925. Both schemes had been drawn up by committees of the League to promote disarmament by providing League members with assurances of immediate military assistance from fellow League members in the event of unprovoked attack.

Britain's reluctance to enter into military commitments on the European mainland after 1919 stemmed partly from reductions in public expenditure which included cuts in the military budget, and partly from her heavy imperial commitments and extra-European responsibilities. While challenges to British imperial rule were increasing, the strength of the British army was declining steadily, from 300,000 men just after the war to 180,000 in the early 1930s. The divisions were not there to give substance to any formal military undertaking to France or to the League unless the government was prepared to cut down on its wider world commitments. Successive British governments opted to maintain, as far as possible, the status and respons-ibilities of a world power even if that meant an inability to guarantee in any tangible way the political settlement in Europe. Ultimately, however, the threat to Britain's security came not from the wider world but from Europe, and a different order of military priorities in the 1920s and early 1930s could well have helped to meet it and so have avoided the build-up to war in 1939. But British governments in the 1920s did not regard Germany as a potential threat to European peace, and were far more concerned about France's refusal to agree to any measures of conciliation, disarmament or treaty revision.

The deadlock between the two governments was broken in early 1925 by a German offer, communicated separately to Britain and France, to enter into an agreement with France for a joint guarantee of their frontiers in western Europe against future aggression. It was suggested that Britain and Belgium should associate themselves with the arrangement. The British Cabinet, having just rejected Chamberlain's suggestion of an Anglo-French alliance, decided to explore the German offer further, and preliminary diplomatic notes were exchanged with the German and French governments. Finally, in September 1925, a conference was held at Locarno in Italy, where a number of agreements were reached. In western Europe, Ger-many, France and Belgium pledged themselves to uphold their existing frontiers and to accept the demilitarized status of the Rhineland. They promised not to resort to force to change the territorial settlement in western Europe, and Britain and Italy agreed to act as guarantors of the pact. In eastern Europe, Germany agreed to a series of arbitration treaties with her neighbours, but, significantly, guarantees were not signed and

Britain and Italy made no agreement to underwrite this part of the European territorial settlement. It was not clear what Britain's obligations would be if an invasion occurred in western Europe as a result of moves in the east to change the territorial settlement there by force.

Locarno was hailed as a great diplomatic triumph. Chamberlain, Briand and Stresemann, who had taken a leading part in the negotiations, were received as national heroes and jointly awarded the Nobel Peace Prize. Their agreement was seen as a milestone on Europe's march to peace and prosperity, and as a result of the negotiations Germany joined the League in 1926. But serious question marks remained. Was Britain's guarantee of the Franco-German and Belgian-German frontiers a firm commitment or an empty gesture of intent, in view of the fact that, at best, only two skeletal British divisions were available to give substance to it? Could the guarantee be readily put into effect, in view of the uncertainty of deciding whether to plan for German or French aggression and in what circumstances? Germany had signified her willingness to accept the Versailles treaty terms relating to western Europe and to the Rhineland. But what about the settlement in eastern Europe? Was she willing to accept that, or would she work to overturn it, perhaps in conjunction with Russia?

From the French point of view, therefore, Locarno was a worrying agreement. It clearly revealed Britain's policy of limited liability for European peace. It marked the largest contribution to French security which the British government was willing to make, and the least the French felt able to accept. And it became clear, after 1925, that it marked only the beginning of Germany's attempts to secure treaty revision and to work systematically to remove one by one the restrictions of the Treaty of Versailles. By 1930, Stresemann was dead and Chamberlain was out of office. Regular meetings between them and Briand had yielded little in the way of agreement over the enforcement or revision of the treaty terms. Depression now engulfed Europe, and mass unemployment fed feelings of frustrated nationalism in Germany. It was increasingly suggested that what could not be obtained by negotiation should be demanded as a matter of right and seized by force. But Britain and France were no nearer to agreement in the early 1930s on how to contain German nationalism than they had been in 1919.

44

Their failure to work together to devise effective policies to implement the peace treaties in the 1920s made it much easier for Nazi leaders to repudiate them without fear of reprisals in the 1930s.

The League of Nations

Given the unstable and impoverished condition of large parts of Europe after 1919, and the growing antagonism between Britain and France, it is hardly surprising that the League, on which so many hopes rested in 1919, should have failed to make a significant political impact. Without the United States and Russia, the League was not a truly world-wide organization, though its membership was numerically impressive. In Japan and Italy it had two leading members intent on pursuing their own expansionist ambitions regardless of the effect this would have on the League or on world peace. Britain and France were left in the 1920s to steer the League through a number of crises and challenges to its authority, and they tried to steer it in diametrically opposing directions. While the French government sought to strengthen League obligations and make them more binding on member states, the British government worked to make them less onerous and more flexible. In the absence of the United States, the British government was extremely concerned that the use of economic sanctions against aggressor nations would only result in a further loss of trade from loyal League members to the United States. Military and naval measures might lead to confrontation with the United States, and would add to Britain's already considerable military burden. In the immediate aftermath of the war, both Britain and France were fully occupied with the problems arising from implementation of the peace treaties, and French leaders were determined to settle these problems directly, or through allied diplomats attending the Conference of Ambassadors which met in Paris throughout the 1920s to deal with issues arising out of the treaties. France was insistent that questions of treaty enforcement should not be considered by the League, and thus the League had to struggle to establish its authority as a major international institution in the years immediately after its formation. Nonetheless, it achieved early success in resolving the Aaland Islands dispute between Sweden and Finland in

1920, when it ruled that the islands should pass into the ownership of Finland. It was less successful in finding a peaceful solution to the dispute between Poland and Lithuania over possession of Vilna, but in 1922 achieved a major economic success with the organization of international financial assistance to rescue Austria from imminent bankruptcy and political collapse. This was followed in the next year by a similar rescue act for Hungary. In the Balkans, a war between Greece and Bulgaria was averted by firm League action in 1925, and much good work was carried out in connection with relief work, the repatriation of prisoners of war, and measures of assistance for refugees and minority groups. In 1927, after an exchange of notes between the American Secretary of State, Kellogg, and Briand of France, the two governments agreed to renounce the use of force in pursuit of their national objectives. This Kellogg Pact was endorsed by fifteen powers in 1928 and there were attempts to weld it to the League Covenant. This did not prove possible, however, and though the conclusion of the pact and its wide adoption seemed to augur well for the maintenance of world peace, there was no enforcement machinery to back it up.

While the League therefore established itself as an international organization capable of resolving disputes between minor powers and promoting a wide range of humanitarian and economic activities, it was not able to deal with the aggressive actions of its leading members. When Italy seized the Greek island of Corfu in 1923, in retaliation for alleged Greek involvement in the murder of an Italian official in Albania, there was no agreement on what action the League should take. France, heavily involved in the Ruhr occupation and desperate for Italian support, did not want to alienate Mussolini. Britain investigated the possibility of taking economic and naval sanctions against Italy, and concluded that they would be difficult to put into effect and hazardous to operate. Meanwhile, Mussolini argued that since the murdered Italian official had been working to demarcate a frontier between Albania and Greece which was part of the overall peace settlement, the crisis should be dealt with not by the League but by the Conference of Ambassadors in Paris. Britain and France accepted this suggestion, and the League was therefore bypassed. As part of the eventual settlement, Italy evacuated Corfu and the Greeks were ordered to pay Italy an indemnity in recompense for the murder, though Greek involvement was never proved. League supporters argued that without the presence of the League in the background, Mussolini would never have agreed to evacuate Corfu. Be that as it may, the League's first attempt to resolve a major crisis was not a resounding success.

When Japan invaded Manchuria in 1931, the League was faced with its second major challenge, at a time when the major European powers were struggling to cope with the effects of the Depression. France was not keen to contemplate military action so far from Europe, and Britain was not willing to agree to economic or naval sanctions against Japan without a firm promise of American support, which was not forthcoming. A League Commission of investigation under Lord Lytton was despatched to the Far East in 1932, but its subsequent report and proposals for a peaceful settlement were ignored by the Japanese. By the end of 1933, Japan was in firm occupation of the whole of Manchuria, and had announced her intention of withdrawing from the League. From this time onwards, Britain and France would have to cope alone with the prospect of Japanese, Italian or German aggression, in the knowledge that they could not count on the active assistance of the United States. It is true that Russia joined the League in 1934, but neither Britain nor France trusted her sufficiently to work closely with her, either in the League or outside. It is hardly surprising that both powers were forced on to the defensive after 1933. The failure of the League to deal effectively with deliberate acts of aggression could hardly inspire confidence for the future, and the prospect of Anglo-French agreement on policies of containment aimed at Germany or Italy seemed dim in view of their record of consistent disagreement in the 1920s. The British government was aware of its military weakness and of its inability to deal simultaneously with German, Italian and Japanese aggression. But rearmament would take time, and was not a politically attractive option in 1933, when the Oxford Union had just declared its unwillingness to fight for King and Country, and a Labour candidate had reversed a National government majority in a sweeping by-election victory in East Fulham, allegedly because of his support for policies of disarmament. France placed her trust in the completion of the Maginot line and in her alliances with Poland and Czechoslovakia, to which she hoped to add an alliance with Russia.

47

However, her leaders were full of dark forebodings about the future and about whether they would be able to respond effectively to aggressive policies aimed at the destruction of the entire peace settlement.

Summary

It was not the Depression that brought the European peace settlement crashing down in ruins. Nor can the peace treaties themselves be blamed for the failure to secure a lasting peace in Europe. As a result of the First World War, Europe was facing serious, deep-seated economic and political problems throughout the 1920s and early 1930s. Those who negotiated the terms of the peace treaties in 1919 did their best to construct a durable settlement, but they disagreed strongly on the best means of achieving this outcome. They were grappling with the forces of nationalism and militarism unleashed by the First World War, and with severe economic dislocation. Any peace settlement framed in such circumstances was bound to suffer from serious shortcomings. But the significant defect of the 1919 settlement did not lie in its terms so much as in the total lack of agreement on how they should be applied, between those who pressed for gradual revision in order to secure the co-operation of the defeated powers and those who believed that peace could only be guaranteed by strict enforcement. Both Britain and France became increasingly frustrated at their inability to modify each other's attitudes and policies, and thus Germany was able to play off one former enemy against the other. By 1933 she had secured substantial revision of the Treaty of Versailles, but it was achieved in a way which caused apprehension in France, irritation in Britain and resentment in Germany. It was clear that German governments would seek further revision, quite possibly by force, and French and British responses to German challenges would be crucial in determining their success or failure. Given the lack of agreement between the two powers on how to deal with German attempts to revise the peace treaties in the 1920s, the outlook in 1933 was not auspicious. The outline of future German challenges could already be forecast. In August, the head of the British Foreign Office, Vansittart, accurately predicted that the new German Chancellor, Adolf

Hitler, would proceed to tear up the clauses of the Treaty of Versailles one by one, and embark on a campaign of eastern expansion. The British government had ample warning, therefore, of the likely course of events, but did not succeed in preventing Hitler from engulfing Britain, and Europe, in war in 1939. The failure of the architects of the 1919 peace settlement to complete their work on an agreed basis in the decade after 1919 was one of the major factors contributing to the outbreak of war just twenty years later.

Peacemaking: the historical debate

The debate on the Paris peace settlement has been conducted largely in two phases. Until the 1950s, view on the achievements of the peace conference and on the resulting treaties – particularly the Treaty of Versailles – were nearly all hostile. The settlement was a bad one; the treaty of Versailles constituted a betrayal of Woodrow Wilson's Fourteen Points and, through their vindictive treatment of Germany, the peacemakers were charged with sowing the seeds for another European conflict. However, the release of a great quantity of government and private papers in the 1950s and 1960s caused a reassessment of the settlement, as did the political problems thrown up by the cold war, such as the complications of arms control agreements and of peace-keeping operations in the 1950s and 1960s, and escalating ethnic tensions in eastern and south-eastern Europe. More detached assessments of the settlement began to appear, arguing that, in the difficult political and economic circumstances of 1918–19, the peacemakers did not do such a bad job. The most recent studies have concluded, indeed, that the settlement was probably the best that could have been achieved, in view of the conflicting pressures and interests amongst the great powers at Paris, and was by no means punitive. Its weaknesses, it has been argued, lay not so much in its terms as in the lack of mechanisms through which to enforce them on a resentful and unchastened Germany.

Not surprisingly, the earliest criticisms of the Treaty of Versailles came from the German delegation which was presented with its draft terms on 7 May 1919. Having had no opportunity to engage in direct negotiations with their former enemies, they immediately denounced the treaty as a betrayal of the Fourteen Points on which they had sued for peace and as being in conflict with truth and national honour. The entire German delegation at Versailles recommended non-acceptance, regardless of the consequences, but the new German government, fearing that a resumption of hostilities would only make matters worse for Germany, decided upon a different strategy. Having been told by the allies that they could furnish written comments on the treaty proposals, they drafted a lengthy set of counter-proposals which were presented both to the peacemakers and to the world's press at the end of May. The Treaty itself was denounced as a 'capitalist peace treaty' which was 'legally and morally untenable and at the same time impracticable'. It would bring about 'the utter destruction of German economic life' and condemn Germany to 'the fate of Russia'. Particularly resented were article 231, immediately denounced as the 'war guilt clause', the denial of self-determination particularly with regard to Germany's eastern frontiers, the proposed cession of Upper Silesia to a reconstituted Poland, exclusion from the League of Nations, and an open-ended reparations bill.

German outrage made an immediate impact at Paris on the British empire delegates, many of whom agreed with the substance of the German complaints. After a lengthy discussion at the beginning of June, it was agreed that Lloyd George should try to persuade his fellow peacemakers to amend the Treaty of Versailles with regard to Germany's eastern frontiers, and in particular Upper Silesia, to reduce the period of allied occupation of the Rhineland, to allow German membership of the League from the outset, and to try to move towards agreement on a fixed reparations total. The only point on which Lloyd George was successful in achieving change was in relation to Upper Silesia, where it was agreed that a plebiscite should take place and that the area should be divided as far as possible along lines of nationality between Germany and Poland. The stubborn attitudes of Wilson and Clemenceau at this point in resisting Lloyd George's suggested changes fuelled British misgivings about the negotiations and the resulting treaty. The chief Treasury delegate, J.M. Keynes, had already resigned in protest at the economic terms and branded the Treaty as 'outrageous and impossible'. Other members of the delegation, including

Smuts and Nicolson, were deeply disillusioned with the outcome of the conference, and the reaction of the Germans to the proposed treaty increased their unhappiness over the whole settlement. Smuts agonised over whether to sign this 'rotten thing of which we shall all be heartily ashamed in due course', this 'thoroughly bad peace', though he finally brought himself to do so. Liberals, radicals and socialists in Britain echoed such sentiments in denouncing the actual peace terms as a far cry from the moral pronouncements of Wilson's Fourteen Points. Beatrice Webb branded the peace settlement as 'hard and brutal' and wrote in her diary, 'We are all so disgusted with the peace that we have ceased to discuss it – one tries to banish it from one's mind as an unclean thing'. Already in May 1919 the *New Statesman* was assuring its readers that 'the settlement will not last'.

In December 1919, six months after the final signing of the Treaty of Versailles, Keynes published a blistering attack on the treaty, and especially on its economic provisions, which echoed many of the earlier German reactions. Not only did he allege that it would be well-nigh impossible for Germany to pay in reparations what was expected of her, but he also accused the peacemakers of 'reducing Germany to servitude for a generation, of degrading the lives of millions of human beings and of depriving a whole nation of happiness', all of which would 'sow the decay of the whole civilised life of Europe'. His critique of the peace settlement, *The Economic Consequences of the Peace*, had an enormous and long-lasting impact, both in Britain and in the United States of America, in turning popular opinion against the Treaty of Versailles on account of its betrayal of Wilson's Fourteen Points and its alleged harsh treatment of Germany. Its vivid portrayals of a vindictive Clemenceau, out for revenge on Germany for defeat in the Franco-Prussian war of 1870–71, of an idealistic but tactically inept and out-manœuvred Wilson, and of an accommodating, unprincipled Lloyd George, out to secure the best short-term deal, left an indelible impression on electorates in Britain and America. The more temperate and detailed six-volume account of *The History of the Peace Conference*, written by participants and historians and edited by Harold Temperley, which appeared between 1920 and 1924, failed to change attitudes in Britain towards the treaty. Many historians, such as A.J.P. Taylor and Martin

Gilbert, have traced the origins of inter-war appeasement in Britain back to 1919 and to guilty consciences over Versailles. Many politicians and commentators in Britain after 1933 saw Hitler's rise to power in Germany as an inevitable consequence of the wrongs of Versailles and were consequently much more willing to accommodate Nazi demands for territorial expansion than they might otherwise have been.

While the overwhelming view in Britain was that the Treaty of Versailles was too harsh on Germany, a large body of French opinion held that it was not harsh enough. Much of the fighting along the Western Front took place on French soil, in a part of France which before 1914 had been extremely productive. Not only had large numbers of Frenchmen been killed, but France's ten richest provinces had been devastated by four years of warfare. In striking contrast, Germany itself had not been invaded. The Treaty of Versailles left it largely intact, with a population almost double that of France, and with no powerful east European neighbours. Such an outcome seemed to many in France to offer Germany the chance for revenge in the not-too-distant future. Right-wing commentators and politicians denounced Wilson's insistence on self-determination, and its effect in fragmenting eastern Europe as 'folly'. On the left, French socialists and communists joined with their counterparts in other European countries in denouncing the treaty as an 'imperialist peace'. As the peace was being signed, Marshall Foch commented, very prophetically, 'This is not peace. It is an armistice for 20 years'. A whole host of French critics, from all political parties, rounded on Clemenceau for having yielded to Anglo-American pressures and compromised vital French interests. In particular, he was criticised for having given up the French claim to a Rhine frontier in exchange for treaties of guarantee from Britain and from the United States of America which then failed to materialize. Within a year of the ending of the conference, Clemenceau had failed to win the French Presidency and had retired from active political life. As many of the intricate compromises he had reluctantly agreed to at Paris fell apart, opinion in France hardened against the treaty's alleged shortcomings, but united in a desire to enforce as much of it as possible. As French leaders watched successive German governments evade its terms, a sense of resigned fatalism took hold. To them, Hitler's rise to power provided further worrying evidence of the inadequacy of the settlement, and raised the chilling prospect of a renewed German military challenge sooner or later.

In Italy, too, the peace settlement was attacked by nationalists as giving inadequate recompense for the sacrifices the war had demanded. Though objectively, Italy had made considerable gains, these fell well short of exaggerated public expectations, particularly in the case of Fiume. The peace was condemned as 'mutilated', and bitter and sustained criticisms helped to undermine the political position of the government and pave the way for the rise to power of Mussolini. In Russia, too, the peace settlement was condemned, but the new Bolshevik regime was confident that conflicts between the victorious 'imperialist powers' could be exploited and that Russia would soon benefit from revolutionary uprisings in Germany and eastern Europe. Such expectations were not dashed until the mid-1920s, and Lenin's successors continued for some time to denounce and to work against the Versailles settlement, whilst at the same time seeking some sort of political and economic accommodation with the major capitalist powers.

In Germany, all parties and sections of society united in their denunciation of the Versailles diktat. Given the domestic difficulties facing the new Weimar republic, political parties could find common ground on few issues, and attacks on the 'iniquitous' peace settlement served to give shaky coalitions some stability and credibility. Versailles was, indeed, 'the unifying bracket that clamped German politics together'. (H. James, from chapter in Kershaw, I. (ed), *Weimar: Why did German Democracy Fail?*) German leaders of all political complexions sought to demonstrate to the allies that it was both unjust and unworkable. German accounts of the peace conference therefore portrayed the peacemakers as vindictive and hypocritical, departing from their own professed principles when it suited them and imposing a punitive peace on the new German regime. The German peace delegation and German radicals who had espoused Wilsonian views were also bitterly attacked for having betrayed the German nation, and a leading delegate at Paris, Matthias Erzberger, having survived one assassination attempt, was murdered by right-wing extremists in August 1921. Much German writing in the 1920s and early 1930s, however, was directed at disproving the notion of sole German

53

war guilt, rather than aimed at the settlement as a whole, in the belief that once Germany's alleged prime responsibility for causing the war was refuted, the treaty itself would lose all validity and would have to be substantially revised.

In the United States, a bitter political battle took place between Woodrow Wilson and his political opponents over the issue of the ratification of the treaty, centring particularly on the obligations and responsibilities America would assume as a member of the League of Nations. In the course of a nation-wide tour to defend the agreements reached at Paris, Wilson suffered a stroke; thereafter, he was not able to prevent the political initiative from passing to his severest critics. They received a further boost from the publication of Keynes's book, which portrayed a rather rigid President being outmanoeuvred on every point of his programme by wily, unscrupulous and more 'street-wise' European leaders. An ill-assorted coalition of Republican and Democratic Senators was successful in blocking the United States of America's ratification of the Treaty of Versailles, with attached reservations, by the required two-thirds majority. However, Wilsons's supporters had already begun a counter-offensive, to portray the President as a man fighting valiantly for the highest ideals, but betrayed on all sides. Wilson's press secretary, Ray Stannard Baker, published a little booklet in November 1919, *What Wilson Did at Paris*, which represented Wilson at the head of the forces of 'New Diplomacy', espousing a rational, just peace negotiated openly and impartially, but being undermined by the rearguard actions of the 'greedy European imperialists' with their insistence on secrecy, territorial guarantees and endless sessions of sordid bartering. While Wilson had been back on home ground in America in February 1919, there had been a 'slump in idealism' in Paris, and all his good work had been undone by the European leaders and by his traitorous confidant, Colonel House.

A year after Baker published his little book, he was entrusted by Wilson with his entire personal files of Peace Conference records. The result was a 3-volume study, *Woodrow Wilson and World Settlement*, published in 1923. Though it was based on copious amounts of primary source material, its main findings repeated and expanded upon the picture drawn in his earlier book, of the New World in conflict with the Old, and of Wilson the crusader battling vainly to bring new ideals and moral precepts into a tired and cynical world. The villains remained the same: Colonel House, too ready to undo the President's work; Clemenceau, distrustful and sceptical; and the unprincipled and untrustworthy Lloyd George. The effect of this publication, and of the debate it provoked both in the United States and in Europe, was to increase criticism of the peace settlement, to confirm belief in the United States that it should on no account allow itself to become involved in the League of Nations or in European affairs, and to stimulate the writing of books rebutting Baker's accusations.

In 1928, an American professor, Charles Seymour, who had been involved in the negotiations at Paris as part of the sizeable United States delegation, published the final two volumes of *The Intimate Papers of Colonel House*, covering the years 1917–1919 and based on diary entries and personal letters. They showed Wilson and House working together very closely up to January 1919, with House being particularly successful in November 1918 in getting the allies to accept Wilson's Fourteen Points as the basis for a peace settlement. Indeed, House emerged from these volumes as an effective negotiator, trying to secure agreement on the basis of Wilson's principles but frequently being frustrated by Wilson's own stubbornness and intransigence. Seymour suggested that it was Wilson himself who brought about the repudiation of the final settlement in the United States, first by compromising with his European colleagues on a number of important and contentious issues in order to secure their agreement to the establishment of a League of Nations, and then by failing to secure the passage of the League Covenant through the Senate.

A more general picture of the tensions and the confusion rife at Paris emerged from the private publication in 1924 of twenty-one volumes of the diary extracts of the chief United States legal adviser, David Hunter Miller. The disclosure of extensive primary source material, both in the diary extracts and in the subsequent two volumes of *The Drafting of the Covenant* (1928), began to reveal the nature of the bargaining and of the constant crises and conflicts of interest at Paris which had made an agreed peace settlement so difficult to reach. Another collection of diary extracts, with an accompanying commentary and verdict on the peace negotiations, was published in Britain in 1933 by Harold Nicolson. Again, conflicting pressures, confusion and compromise were prominent themes. Nicolson mourned the inability of the peacemakers to adhere to Wilson's high ideals, while faithfully charting all the obstacles in the way of a just and wise peace. As a delegate, he had roundly condemned the reparations clauses. 'The great crime', he had written to his wife in May 1919, 'is in the reparations clauses, which were drawn up solely to please the House of Commons, and which are quite impossible to execute.' However, by 1933, he had come to the conclusion that 'Given the atmosphere of the time, given the passions aroused in all democracies by four years of war, it would have been impossible even for supermen to devise a peace of moderation and righteousness.' And, as his extracts and commentary revealed, though the peacemakers were well-meaning, sincere and able politicians, they were no supermen.

Meanwhile, Lloyd George was busy putting together his own recollections of events at Paris. In the mid-1930s, he published several volumes of *War Memoirs*, followed by a two-volume study, *The Truth About the Peace Treaties*. Not surprisingly, the former prime minister emerged from these publications as a far-sighted leader, wanting to punish the Germans for their un-provoked aggression in 1914 and for war crimes committed in the course of the war, but also concerned to moderate some of the harsh French and United States proposals, particularly in relation to the eastern frontier between Poland and Germany. Lloyd George documented in great detail his attempts to secure modifications in the draft treaty, particularly over Upper Silesia and German membership of the League, and Wilson's refusal to contemplate any substantial changes at that time. Lloyd George portrayed himself as idealistic, a supporter of the new League of Nations, but only if it was based on the firm foundations of Anglo-American understanding and agreement about levels of armament and mandate responsibilities, which, he claimed, the Americans were reluctant to accept. Lloyd George's publica-tions began to appear in the mid-1930s when Europe seemed to be moving once again to the brink of war, with the contentious eastern frontiers referred to by Lloyd George fuelling strong German demands for revision and for expansion. Unkind critics could – and did – suggest that one of Lloyd George's main aims in publishing his memoirs was not to present an accurate account of the peace negotiations but to shift the blame for the highly dangerous contemporary European situation away from himself. One such critic, Lord Hardinge, who had been Permanent Under-Secretary at the British Foreign Office between 1916 and 1920, claimed that the peace treaties 'contained provisions which anybody with any knowledge of foreign politics or of European affairs would have realized as being opposed to every principle of national life and existence' and that the responsibility for them rested 'principally with Lloyd George'. In his memoirs, *Old Diplomacy*, which were published in 1947, soon after both the Second World War and Lloyd George's death, he accused Lloyd George of ignoring the advice of his experts at Paris and of listening to anybody 'whose views might coincide with his own, whether they really knew anything of the subject or not'. Hardinge, of course, was no impartial observer, and the hostility of the trained diplomat towards someone he regarded as an amateur and inept peacemaker was heartily reciprocated by Lloyd George, whose view of diplomats had been that they 'were invented simply to waste time'.

By the 1950s, most of those who had been active participants at Paris had died, and criticisms of the peace settlement had ceased to be a central element of current political debate. The release of large quantities of British and United States documents, along with a series of new crises generated by cold war, helped to change perspectives and views. Wilson's peace programme was attacked in the United States by a school of 'realists' which included Hans Morganthau and George Kennan, not because of his failure to realize it, but because of its impracticability and in particular its neglect of national interests and failure to recognize the need for compromise with other states. Scholarly studies of particular elements of peace-making, such as Nelson's *Land and Power: British and Allied Policy on Germany's Frontiers, 1916–19* (published in 1963) and Seth Tillman's examination of *Anglo-American Relations at the Peace Conference* (1961), showed up clearly the divergent interests of the participants at Paris and the complicated nature of the compromises, which, of necessity, had to be fashioned through exhaustive and detailed negotiations.

Writing in the *New Cambridge Modern History* volume dealing with late nineteenth- and twentieth-century European history, which appeared in 1964, Rohan Butler argued that on Germany's eastern frontier, a 'creditably fair compromise' was in fact reached, and that the Germans, to divert attention away from their own 'greedy and vindictive war aims', launched an instant, and very effective, propaganda campaign against the proposed treaty, and in particular against the so-called 'war guilt clause'. This clause had actually been inserted in the treaty, Butler pointed out, to establish and then limit Germany's financial liabilities, in yet another of the Paris compromises reached to try to resolve the divergent views of the United States, Britain and France. But it had been plucked out of the financial section of the treaty by the German delegation and instantly denounced as a clause unfairly placing moral war guilt on the German nation. Butler conceded that the treaty was a severe imposition upon the new democratic Weimar republic and commented that 'seldom has so stringent a treaty been framed with such idealistic intent'. Nonetheless, he saw the main problems with the settlement as arising not so much from the treaties themselves but from the fact that the Germans never accepted that they had suffered defeat, that the war had left a dangerous power vacuum in eastern Europe, and that the struggle to restore stability in Europe was further undermined by the United States withdrawal from the implementation of the settlement after 1920. He also drew attention to the psychological effects of the war in bringing about a retreat from the principles of liberalism and in helping to unleash the forces of communism, fascism and Nazism, which in their turn contributed to the continuing instability of inter-war Europe.

Writing in 1972, Howard Elcock, in his *Portrait of a Decision: The Council of Four and the Treaty of Versailles*, shared Butler's view that the post-war withdrawal of the United States from Europe's political affairs, together with the catastrophic slump of 1929, destroyed any chance the Versailles settlement might have had of working. His study, focused on the world's first political 'summit meeting', the Council of Four which met at Paris between March and the end of April, 1919, not only considered the nature and shape of the compromises reached, but examined the importance of domestic political pressures on the leaders, the complications of wartime secret diplomacy, and the growing threat of Bolshevism. Lloyd George, Clemenceau and Wilson had no established political models of procedure to follow, Elcock argued, and were forced to improvise a framework through which a peace could be negotiated. In the circumstances, they operated quite effectively, and the failure of the settlement did not lie so much in the deficiencies of their work as in what happened *after* 1919.

In two major studies published in 1959 and 1967, *Political Origins of the New Diplomacy* and *Politics and Diplomacy of Peacemaking*, the United States historian Arno Mayer had already highlighted the importance of the Bolshevik challenge, and Wilson's response, in the process of peacemaking. He argued vigorously that the real leitmotiv running through all the proceedings at the Paris peace conference was fear of the spread of Bolshevism and a determination to contain it by any means possible. However, more recent historical studies have not endorsed this view, arguing that it was the German problem rather than the Russian one which most exercised the peacemakers, though the Bolshevik menace was a serious and wearying background preoccupation.

By the mid-1970s, the efforts of the peacemakers were being viewed with increasing sympathy and understanding by historians. In *The Illusion of Peace: International Relations in Europe, 1918–1933*, Sally Marks argued that, given the circumstances prevailing in the immediate aftermath of the war, the divergent interests of the powers involved, and the haphazard nature of the proceedings at Paris, it was remarkable that the Treaty of Versailles was not much more unsatisfactory than it in fact was. The problem was not that the Treaty itself was exceptionally unfair but that the Germans thought it was and directed their efforts, very successfully, to persuading others that it was. The compromise reached between Wilsonian idealism and French cynicism soon proved to be unworkable, though Marks pointed out that even a Wilsonian peace would have involved some territorial loss to Poland and would therefore have been unacceptable to Germany. The main problem was that the peace left Germany both powerful and resentful, with a string of weak neighbours to her east, fearful of her future intentions. Negotiating the treaty was only the first step. The more important task was to enforce it, and it was here, argued Marks, that the peacemakers really failed.

This was a point also highlighted by A.J.P. Taylor in his controversial publication of 1961, *The Origins of the Second World War*, when he observed that 'the treaty was designed to provide security against a new German aggression, yet it could work only with the cooperation of the German government'. Under the Treaty of Versailles, Germany was to help bring about her own disarmament, was to co-operate in the payment of reparations, and was to assist an allied army of occupation. If she refused to work with the allies in the execution of the treaty, how could the treaty be enforced? As Taylor noted, Germany after 1919 remained 'by far the greatest Power on the continent of Europe; with the disappearance of Russia, more so than before. She was greatest in population ... her preponderance was greater still in the economic resources of coal and steel.' Once she recovered from the effects of the war, she would constitute a major threat to the other continental European powers, and the settlement contained nothing that would effectively guard against this situation.

In his study of *Guilt at Versailles*, published in 1984, Anthony Lentin observed that 'it was a wise precept of Machiavelli that the victor should either conciliate his enemy or destroy him' and that the Treaty of Versailles did neither. 'It did not pacify Germany, still less permanently weaken her ... but left her scourged, humiliated and resentful. It was neither a Wilson Peace nor a Clemenceau peace, but a witches' brew concocted of the least palatable ingredients of each' which ultimately were ineffective because 'they cancelled each other out'. While Lentin was critical of Wilson, whom he saw as making a succession of momentous and in the end irreparable errors of judgement and tactics, and of the opportunistic Lloyd George, forever seeking to satisfy a whole range of divergent domestic interests, the fundamental problem remained a powerful and unrepentant Germany, unable to come to terms with the fact that she had lost the war. Not only had Germany come close to the military subjugation of Europe, but she had emerged from the war in better shape than her neighbours and late enemies. The French were only too conscious of this fact, but the view in Britain was rather of a Germany which had been treated too harshly at Paris, and of a treaty that would soon require substantial modification in Germany's favour. As Lentin has recently argued, because the peace settlement was seen on all sides as such an unsatisfactory compromise, there was 'little will to enforce Versailles on the American and British side, little confidence in its effectiveness on the French side, and on the part of Germany, every inducement to undermine it'. Not surprisingly, therefore, the settlement proved to be ineffective in establishing a lasting peace.

The most recent comprehensive study of peacemaking, published in 1991 by Alan Sharp, *The Versailles Settlement: Peacemaking in Paris, 1919*, draws on the full range of documentation now available to the historian relating to the problems and potential negotiating strategies involving the delegations of all the participating nations. He also draws attention to the major unresolved political problems and new challenges arising from the late war. Given all the circumstances, Sharp emphasises the impossibility of the size of the task facing the peacemakers in 1919 in endeavouring to 're-shape the world, the nature of states and international relations in a new image' and to redeem all their wartime pledges. He saw the peacemakers as being 'as much the victims of their virtues as their vices' and concluded that the peace conference witnessed an inevitable series of compromises as the 'needs of security, economic and political stability, nationalism and justice all vied with each other'. While individual leaders had their faults and made their share of mistakes and misjudgements, they were working in a highly charged and unstable environment which was constantly threatening to undo their work. Sharp has rightly reminded us of one of the most important facts about the post-war situation, that 'by the time it ended in 1918, the war had solved few of the problems which had created it. It had, in some cases, dramatically changed their form and increased their complexity, and it had added to their number. Its length and intensity produced an unpromising atmosphere in which to attempt to resolve these accumulated difficulties.' In 1919 there was still a 'German problem', there was still a 'nationalities problem' in eastern and south-eastern Europe, which had 'emerged in a startling new form', there was an ongoing Eastern Question, there was the problem of who would meet the massive bill for fighting the war, and there was a new and virulent strain of Russian menace. No wonder peacemaking was such a complex and exhausting process!

Current views about the Treaty of Versailles therefore differ considerably from earlier assessments. The great majority of British, German, French and American historians now generally agree that the treaty was, in Niall Ferguson's words, 'relatively lenient', that it was, as the German historian Hillgrüber asserts, 'too weak to be a "Carthaginian peace"' (i.e. very harsh), and that, as the French historian Soutou comments, it 'would not have been easy' for the peacemakers 'to do much better'. The leading personalities at Paris have been subjected to intense scrutiny, and both Clemenceau and Lloyd George are now viewed as having emerged from the peacemaking process with some credit, fighting both to safeguard the interests of their countries and to construct a durable and rational peace. It is Woodrow Wilson who has increasingly been seen as having failed to negotiate effectively, both in terms of his inability to deal with domestic opposition to his policies and in terms of his intransigence at vital points of discussion at Paris.

No part of the Paris peace settlement has been more vigorously debated than the reparations clauses, and, again, modern assessments of the weight of the burden actually placed on Germany differ greatly from the picture drawn in 1919 by Keynes. The first sustained challenge to Keynes's critique came just after the Second World War, in a book by a young French economist, Etienne Mantoux, who was tragically killed in the last weeks of that conflict. *The Carthaginian Peace* set out to demonstrate that Keynes was wrong when he concluded that it was economically impossible for Germany to execute the reparations clauses of the Versailles Treaty, and to this end Mantoux challenged most of Keynes's central arguments. Germany's tremendous economic and military revival in the 1930s, he argued, demonstrated the underlying strength of the German economy, and the great recovery it had already made by 1929 showed that the Treaty was not economically punitive or vindictive. Indeed, Mantoux asserted, the Reparations Commission after 1920 went out of its way to help Germany to fulfil its reparation obligations with the least possible pain, while successive German governments tried to dodge all payments and to dispute the whole legality of payment. Mantoux also calculated that while 35–8 milliard marks flowed into Germany in the form of loans, mainly short-term, between 1920 and 1931, Germany only paid to the allies in that period 21 milliard marks, thus enabling her to re-equip factories and expand and modernize her industries. Mantoux noted, finally, that the catastrophic depreciation of the mark in the early 1920s, which caused so much hardship to ordinary German people, was the result not of the so-called 'reparations burden' but of runaway inflation resulting from the financing of the war itself and the handling of the accrued debt, and he pointed out that the kind of financial and exchange controls introduced by the Nazi government after 1933 could have been employed by Weimar governments to stabilize the economic situation in Germany.

While Mantoux's book did not rival Keynes's in terms of immediate impact or huge sales, its arguments have been supported and reinforced in more recent historical writing. Sally Marks, an American historian who has written extensively on reparations issues in the 1920s, believes that 'the scholarly consensus now suggests that paying what was actually asked of her was within Germany's capacity'. German governments in the early 1920s could have followed the example of the French government after the Franco-Prussian war of 1870–1, which made considerable efforts to pay off the sizeable war indemnity demanded by Germany within a few years. They could, had they so wished, have increased their low rates of tax, have raised domestic loans in order to pay off the reparations sums demanded, and, as a consequence, have secured the removal of the occupying Allied troops from the Rhineland. Instead, they treated the reparation issues as part of an ongoing political battle with their former enemies, in, as one German official at the time put it, 'the continuation of war by other means'. In Sally Marks' words, 'As France and Germany both understood, but Britain and America rarely seemed to, reparations constituted the primary battlefield in the continuing contest over who won the war and over whether Germany would again dominate the continent.' All combatants, and in particular France and Belgium, faced huge reconstruction costs. France's ten richest provinces had been devastated by four years of warfare and by deliberate German sabotage of factories and mines as the German army retreated back to Germany. If Germany evaded the payment of substantial sums in reparation, while France had to restore the war damage she suffered by utilizing her own resources, this would be a considerable step towards German economic and political recovery in Europe.

Thus historians now recognize that from the early 1920s reparations became the 'chief battleground of the post-war era, the focus of the power struggle between France and Germany over whether the Versailles Treaty was to be enforced or revised'. And in that struggle, both Britain and the United States deserted their wartime ally and gave considerable support to Germany. Both countries were concerned to return as soon as possible to pre-war international economic arrangements, resting on stable foreign exchange mechanisms and the gold standard. If Germany could be assisted to pay reparations as speedily as possible, and if war debts owed to the United States could be settled by agreement, then the economic problems bequeathed by the war would disappear and both nations could resume their profitable world-wide trading. However, the economic damage caused by the war could not be mended so easily. It had cost the allied and associated powers two and a half times as much to win the war as it had cost the Central Powers to lose it. Britain and France spent the 1920s servicing huge war debts which consumed between a third and a half of their annual budgets. They therefore sought American help and in particular the extension of credit to bring about an economic recovery in Europe. However, the United States would only help Europe if it showed evidence of political stability and of burying wartime animosities, and France's increasingly desperate attempts to secure reparations from Germany, culminating in the disastrous Ruhr occupation, confirmed the worst suspicions of United States politicians and businessmen that European powers were out to secure American finance to further their own selfish national interests.

The Ruhr invasion of 1923–4, which triggered off the spectacular collapse in value of the German mark, finally brought about United States intervention in Europe's economic affairs, but as one American historian, William MacDougall, observed in *France's Rhineland Diplomacy 1914–24* (1978), United States policy in the Dawes Plan consisted of 'financing Germany's return to industrial dominance, lending her far more than she would pay in reparations, while simultaneously squeezing France to pay her war debts, disarm and hasten the dismantling of Versailles'. France is now seen by historians as having been badly treated by her allies after 1919, left to restore her war-torn provinces and weakened economy as best she could, and forced to battle with Germany alone for the reparations due to her. Her suggestions for schemes of broad economic co-operation, involving her war-time partners, as well as Germany, and in some respects foreshadowing post-1945 developments, were rejected by Britain and the United States, neither of whom wished to be financially or militarily involved in ongoing European schemes which might necessitate security obligations to France. Her invasion of the Ruhr is now seen by historians as evidence of France's growing weakness and isolation, a desperate act to seize the reparations due to her and to try to strangle the inexorable German political and economic recovery and prevent a further military confrontation.

British reparations policy, meanwhile, has come in for considerable criticism. Trachtenberg, in *Reparation in World Politics* (1980), pointed out that, due partly to domestic pressures, 'throughout the period of the peace conference, Great Britain was to pursue a reparations policy more demanding and more intransigent than the policy of any other allied Power'. It was Lloyd George who tripled the size of the final bill by arguing that reparations should include pension payments and allowances due to servicemen, incurred as a result of the war, to increase the share of the spoils that Britain could claim. It was Lloyd George also who was instrumental in a whole series of ingenious compromises to fix Germany's reparations liability without mentioning a sum in the treaty, and to postpone detailed discussions until after the conference. The 'war guilt' clause, formulated as part of the complex financial settlement, was only one, though clearly the most powerful, of the weapons which the Versailles reparations settlement handed to the Germans. And the greater the fuss the Germans made about the alleged iniquities of the treaty and of its financial provisions, the more concerned British governments became to revise the treaty – though invariably at France's expense.

Most historians of the Paris peace conference now take the view that, in economic terms, the treaty was not unduly harsh on Germany and that, while obligations and damages were inevitably much stressed in the debates at Paris to satisfy electors reading the daily newspapers, the intention was quietly to give Germany substantial help towards paying her bills, and to meet many of the German objections by amendments to the way the reparations schedule was in practice carried out. In terms of war damage, historians now stress that Germany was one of the luckier belligerents, in the sense that she emerged with her economy intact and 'was spared invasion, denudation and devastation'. As the American historian Stephen Shuker observed, in *The End of French Predominance* (1976), 'Significantly,

Germany emerged from World War I despite military defeat less damaged in terms of human and economic resources than the other major European combatants.'

It was indeed this German strength, rather than weakness, which brought about such a strong German reaction to the Treaty. The German nation had not been invaded, and the troops had returned home in good order, had been welcomed at festive receptions and had been greeted as 'undefeated heroes'. The authorities in Germany commended the bravery of those soldiers who had 'stood their ground undefeated up to the last minute'. Germany did not feel herself to be a defeated nation. An armistice had been sought on the basis of Wilson's Fourteen Points peace programme because this offered the best chance of a lenient peace and would enable military leaders, businessmen and politicians to minimize the consequences of a defeat that had never seriously been contemplated until the autumn of 1918. Historians who have studied German primary source material point out that German leaders were discussing the anticipated peace terms, including the likelihood of a charge of war guilt and a substantial reparations bill, before they were presented with the final treaty, and were formulating various strategies through which they could maximize their bargaining power and minimize treaty obligations. The newly appointed foreign secretary, Brockdorff-Rantzau, strongly believed that Germany remained a great world power with considerable economic strength and that he could use this strength to bargain with the allies to achieve a settlement in which losses of territory would be minimal and Germany would become a founder member of the Council of the League of Nations, would keep all her overseas colonies and would undertake only limited reconstruction obligations in France and Belgium. Brockdorff-Rantzau's illusions about the likely strength of Germany's bargaining position at the peace conference were shared by many colleagues, industrialists, bankers and army officers.

Thus when the treaty was finally presented, Germany was ready with denunciations, some prepared and some spontaneous. The Germans found a war guilt clause, though it was buried in the reparations section of the treaty at clause 231, and they elevated its significance far beyond the narrow intentions of those who had formulated the clause initially. They found large-scale reparations, though unspecified in total amount, which they claimed would impoverish the nation. They were enraged by territorial losses, particularly to Poland, by the loss of all colonies, by the stringent disarmament provisions and by the occupation of the Rhineland. And they were frustrated and embittered by the fact that the allies, apart from Lloyd George, showed no desire to engage in further negotiations with them.

Clearly, German expectations about the peace process in 1919 and about the likely nature of the final settlement were completely unrealistic. They failed to take into account the domestic pressures on the allied peacemakers, the tremendous sense of weakness felt by the French at the end of a war of attrition in which they had been rescued from defeat by their overseas allies and associates, and the difficult process of adjusting conflicting interests on the allied side. Unfortunately, the allies were equally unrealistic in assuming that Germany would co-operate in carrying out the peace terms. As historians now acknowledge, the real criticism of the peace settlement lies not so much in its terms as in its lack of means of enforcement. Peacemakers were well aware that German power in 1919 had to be curbed, but they naïvely assumed that Germany would accept the Versailles medicine handed to them, just as France had complied with stringent peace terms in 1871 after the Franco-Prussian war. Instead, the Germans took every opportunity to denounce the settlement, declare it morally invalid because it contravened Wilson's Fourteen Points, and seek to subvert or substantially revise it. And in this strategy, they soon acquired considerable support from the British government.

Peacekeeping: the problems

Just as present-day historians take a much more sympathetic view of the problems faced by the peacemakers in 1919, they are also far less likely to place on them the blame for the international instability which plagued Europe in the inter-war period and for the outbreak of a further world war in 1939. Recent research has made much clearer the debilitating effect of the First World War on much of Europe, and the relative loss of power of France and Britain. Both these powers are now seen as being very much on the defensive after 1919, and seeking to maintain their world influence and economic power in the face of aggressive challenges from the United States and Japan and the ideological threat of the new Soviet Union. It was their inability to reconcile conflicting interests, and the United States' reluctance to help to rehabilitate Europe and particularly the new successor states of the East, which, it is now argued, facilitated a renewed German challenge for the mastery of Europe, a challenge which the peace settlement of 1919 was too weak to contain.

Studies of the impact of the First World War on all the participants have revealed the wide-ranging political, social, economic and psychological extent of the conflict. Perhaps because the magnitude and duration of the war were so unexpected, the psychological effects were considerable, particularly in Britain. Attempts have been made to calculate the total costs of the war in various ways, either by estimating its overall economic costs or by estimating the amount of economic loss suffered by the belligerents, or by showing what structural economic changes the war brought about. Recent research has clearly showed that two significant economic effects of the war were, first, the loss by European powers of overseas markets bringing a marked reduction in their share of world trade, and, second, the forced sale by Britain and France of a substantial proportion of their pre-war foreign investments, about 25 per cent in the case of Britain and about 50 per cent in that of France. By contrast, as Herdach points out in *The First World War, 1914–18* (1977), the United States emerged from the war as a major creditor nation with increased foreign investments, and New York stood poised to replace London as the financial capital of the world. This development was potentially serious for Europe, for whereas before 1914 the international economy thrived on Britain's free-trade policies, after 1919 the world's new leading financial power continued to build on a tradition of protectionist policies designed to safeguard the home market. Thus the attempts of European trading powers to gain access to the world's largest market or to recapture lost markets were likely to prove very difficult.

Socially and politically the war had far-reaching and sometimes completely unexpected effects, as the social historian Jay Winter has shown in *The Great War and the British People* (1985) and Jurgen Kocka has explored in *Facing Total War: German Society 1914–18* (1973). Not all developments were bad; some social groups made significant gains in the course of the war, particularly working-class people and most women, but this only created further problems after 1919 when those who had lost influence or position tried to regain it. The war also left behind large numbers of widows and dependents who looked to state support for their economic survival, but whose economic interests conflicted with those of more wealthy citizens who complained about heavy tax burdens. Recent research has highlighted the areas of social conflict which the war helped to create and which then caused considerable domestic instability across Europe in the 1920s.

Social conflicts assumed even greater importance after the two Russian Revolutions of 1917. The new Bolshevik regime was intent on fanning revolutionary fires across Europe and used the latest communications technology of the day to spread its ideological message. As well as facing an American challenge, therefore, the European great powers were on the defensive against Bolshevism, which aroused fears amongst more affluent social classes of the imminent collapse of civilized life. At the same time, the collapse of the Hapsburg and Ottoman empires in 1918 had brought fragmentation and disorder to east and south-east Europe.

The peace conference was therefore held at a time of unprecedented political, social, economic and ideological upheaval. Any peace settlement would have to operate within highly unstable international and domestic environments, and it is recognized much more clearly now by historians than it was by contemporaries that it was this international instability, coupled with a whole series of intractable domestic problems faced by individual European countries, rather than the particular provisions of the peace settlement itself which made the attainment of a lasting peace so difficult.

In this difficult international climate, Britain and France struggled to find ways of conciliating or containing Germany, while at the same time preserving their own power. For Britain, this meant securing a release from European obligations as quickly as possible in order to concentrate on the consolidation of colonial power and the revival of world-wide trade. For France, however, it required the construction of a series of alliances with east European states to replace the pre-war Russo-French alliance which had so effectively encircled Germany and a guarantee from Britain that she would come to France's aid if

France should be the victim of unprovoked attack. Thus the two powers were bent on very different strategies for dealing with Germany; as Alan Sharp has aptly remarked, while the British government saw 66 million potential German customers, the French government trembled at the prospect of 66 million German soldiers and possible invaders.

Recent historians have shown great sympathy for Britain's plight in the immediate aftermath of the war. Her imperial commitments had expanded, particularly in Africa and the Middle East, as a result of the new League of Nations mandates system. However, her capacity to discharge them had markedly declined. In *The Realities of Diplomacy* (1981) and *The Rise and Fall of British Naval Mastery* (1977), Paul Kennedy argued very persuasively that the foundations of Britain's world power had been considerably eroded by 1919, not only because of the war but also because of the rise of economic rivals and the changing requirements of new technologies. Not only had British power been under challenge before 1914 from the United States and Germany, but at home, the greatly expanded electorate after 1918 was demanding social, rather than military, expenditure. European commitments were expensive and would necessitate extra military spending at a time when war debts were forcing cuts in government spending. Furthermore, they were unpopular with electors, many of whom believed that it was the secret diplomatic agreements entered into by Sir Edward Grey before 1914 which had dragged Britain into war.

Thus Britain had little room for diplomatic manoeuvre after 1919; her aim was to preserve the powers and possessions she had, to seek peace, to reduce government spending, particularly on armaments, and to revive trade. Some historians, notably Corelli Barnett in *The Collapse of British Power* (1972), argue that Britain was not greatly weakened in 1919, and that she could have pursued a more vigorous and active set of European and international policies which might have prevented war in 1939, but this is now a minority view. Detailed studies, particularly of naval disarmament conferences and of Anglo-American diplomacy in the 1920s, show the extent to which Britain's world-wide interests were coming under pressure from the United States and the growing difficulty of protecting them.

At the same time, France was attempting to construct a network of European alliances in anticipation of the next military confrontation with Germany. French inter-war policies are no longer seen as provocative but as profoundly defensive, with successive French governments trying vainly to secure a replacement from Britain for the abortive Anglo-American treaties of guarantee. French leaders were acutely aware of Germany's evasions of her treaty obligations, of secret deals with Russia and of the fact that Germany would have to be forced by the allies to comply with the peace terms. France also knew how reluctant Britain would be to support such tactics and how important British aid would be to France in any further conflict. French leaders therefore faced a series of dilemmas during the 1920s; France had to try to gain support from Britain, but not at the cost of substantial treaty revision, and to continue her policies of containment of Germany, while at the same time being faced with increasing rivalry from another neighbour, Italy, under its new Fascist leader, Mussolini.

The traditional view of 1920s European diplomacy is that the period of unrest which culminated in the Ruhr occupation and the American-sponsored reparations settlement was brought to an end by the Locarno conference of 1925, which ushered in a period of relative tranquillity. Recent research has challenged this interpretation and has suggested that the deep-seated problems which Europe was facing after 1919 were not resolved by the Locarno settlement. Jon Jacobson, in *Locarno Diplomacy: Germany and the West, 1925–9* (1972), explored post-Locarno diplomacy and negotiations in great depth and concluded that 'although certain questions regarding security, disarmament, demilitarisation and reparations were . . . partially resolved between 1924 and 1929, fundamental rivalries and antagonisms persisted through the Locarno era'. Most significantly, 'Stresemann, Briand and Chamberlain came to no agreement about the place of Germany in Europe, and not having settled this question, the Locarno powers did not cease to threaten each other.' There was no follow-up to Locarno in any other troubled region of Europe. Germany, most significantly, did not make binding agreements concerning her eastern frontiers. As far as an understanding between Britain and France was concerned, Locarno was 'the most the British would offer and the least the French would accept.' There could be no binding Anglo-French military agreements on the basis of the Locarno agreements, as no action could be decided upon in advance of knowing who the

71

aggressor was, France or Germany. Furthermore, at the time of the conclusion of the Locarno treaties, Britain had only two skeletal divisions available for European action and clearly therefore could not be counted on to take decisive action, whoever the aggressor.

Could the newly established League of Nations have been used more vigorously by its leading powers to bring about peace in Europe? League of Nations enthusiasts in Britain, such as Lord Robert Cecil and Professor Gilbert Murray, argued that a more committed League policy on the part of Britain in the inter-war period could have proved an effective alternative to dis-credited 'balance of power' policies, and that whole-hearted League policies of disarmament, combined with added pro-visions of security, could have averted another war. However, more recent research into French and British Foreign Office records, and considerable experience of the operation of the League's successor body, the United Nations, suggest that this is a very naïve view. Members of the League of Nations did not abandon their foreign policy objectives when they travelled to Geneva; instead, they sought to achieve their objectives through the League. Thus Geneva became one more battleground on which the British and French delegates fought out their conflict-ing strategies for European pacification in the 1920s and early 1930s. Britain pressed for disarmament, France for security, and each power gathered around it a number of supporters. Thus the League was unable to operate effectively either to resolve conflict or to promote disarmament, and once Germany joined the organization, as a result of the Locarno treaties, agreements proved even more difficult to reach. There has been some debate about the impact of American repudiation of the League, and about whether American membership might have helped to strengthen the powers of the League. However, as the present author has argued in *The League of Nations* (1973), the United States did not join the League precisely because a majority of Senators insisted that she should only subscribe to the Covenant with reservations, safeguarding the liberty of the United States to act unilaterally in certain situations. Thus a League with the United States amongst its members might well have faced even greater conflicts of national interest and even more difficulty in reaching agreement on a range of problems. George Egerton in *Great Britain and the Creation of the League of Nations* (1979), demonstrated clearly the very different conceptions of international organization held by the British, French and United States delegates at Paris, and the disappointment all felt with different aspects of the final Covenant. There was no way that the League could help to resolve the problems facing Europe in the 1920s; all it could do was to reflect them.

Some armament limitation agreements were successfully negotiated in the 1920s, but again recent research has shown how painfully compromises were hammered out and how what were considered to be straightforward issues could suddenly produce complications and demands for trade-offs. Thus, in the field of international organization and disarmament, historians now stress not cynicism and a determination to sabotage new diplomacy and revert to the old, but honest endeavour in a very new environment.

Thus the overall emphasis amongst historians studying the 1920s is no longer on alleged missed opportunities at the Paris peace conference, but on the intractable difficulties facing policy-makers after 1919. Respective prime ministers and foreign secretaries still have their critics, but they also have large numbers of defenders, ready to point to the dilemmas and difficulties facing governments in the different European countries. Perhaps the most criticism is now reserved for the very cautious and often negative United States policies which are compared unfavourably with the country's much more successful policies of the post-1945 period. However, while historians agree on the magnitude of the problems facing Europe's leaders in the 1920s, caused both by the war and by the conflicting interests of the major powers, they do not go on to draw the conclusion that a Second World War was therefore inevitable. There was undoubtedly a 'German problem' in Europe in the 1920s which remained unresolved, but the ensuing Depression and the growth of extremism in Germany were not easy to forecast, and the coming to power of Hitler was by no means inevitable. Thus, while Europe was certainly not pacified in the years before the Depression, some crises had been resolved, and the prospect of war did seem to be slowly receding. It was the disastrous economic effects of the Depression in the early 1930s which plunged Europe once more into chaos, and opened up many of the wounds which had been slowly healing since 1919.

Appendix One

The powers represented at Paris

1 *Powers with general interests*
British Empire, France, Italy, Japan, United States.
2 *Powers with special interests*
Australia, Belgium, Brazil, Canada, China, Cuba, the Czecho-slovak Republic, Greece, Guatemala, Haiti, Hedjaz (later Saudi Arabia), Honduras, India, Liberia, New Zealand, Nicaragua, Panama, Poland, Portugal, Romania, Serbia, Siam, South Africa.
3 *Powers with a right of attendance at sessions affecting them*
Bolivia, Ecuador, Peru, Uruguay.

Appendix Two

A summary of Woodrow Wilson's Fourteen Points

1 Open covenants of peace, openly arrived at, after which there shall be no private international understandings of any kind.
2 Absolute freedom of navigation upon the seas . . . alike in peace and in war.
3 The removal, so far as possible, of all economic barriers.
4 Adequate guarantees given and taken that national armaments will be reduced to the lowest point consistent with domestic safety.
5 A free, open-minded and impartial adjustment of all colonial claims, based upon a strict observance of the principle that the interests of the population concerned must have equal weight with the equitable claims of the government whose title is to be determined.
6 The evacuation of all Russian territory and . . . a settlement of all questions affecting Russia.
7 Belgium . . . must be evacuated and restored.
8 All French territory should be freed and the invaded portions restored, and the wrong done to France by Prussia in 1871 in the matter of Alsace Lorraine . . . should be righted.
9 A readjustment of the frontiers of Italy should be effected along clearly recognizable lines of nationality.

10 The peoples of Austria-Hungary . . . should be accorded the freest opportunity of autonomous development.
11 Romania, Serbia and Montenegro should be evacuated; occupied territories restored; Serbia accorded free and secure access to the sea; . . . and international guarantees of the political and economic independence and territorial integrity of the several Balkan States should be entered into.
12 The Turkish portions of the present Ottoman empire should be assured a secure sovereignty, but the other nationalities which are now under Turkish rule should be assured . . . an absolutely unmolested opportunity of autonomous development, and the Dardanelles should be permanently opened as a free passage to the ships and commerce of all nations under international guarantees.
13 An independent Polish State should be erected which should include the territories inhabited by indisputably Polish populations, which should be assured a free and secure access to the sea.
14 A general association of nations must be formed under specific covenants for the purposes of affording mutual guarantees of political independence and territorial integrity to great and small states alike.

Select Bibliography

Place of publication is London unless otherwise stated

Books on the peace negotiations

P. Birdsall, *Versailles Twenty Years After* (1941).

R. Butler, 'The Peace Settlement of Versailles 1918–1933' in *The New Cambridge Modern History, vol XII: The Shifting Balance of World Forces* (1968).

M. Dockrill and D. Goold, *Peace Without Promise: Britain and the Peace Conference 1919–23* (1981).

H. Elcock, *Portrait of a Decision: The Council of Four and the Treaty of Versailles* (1972).

J.M. Keynes, *The Economic Consequences of the Peace* (1919); reprinted as vol. 2 of *Collected Writings* (1971).

I. Lederer, *The Versailles Settlement* (New Jersey, 1961).

A. Lentin, *Guilt at Versailles: Lloyd George and the Pre-History of Appeasement* (1985).

D. Lloyd George, *The Truth about the Peace Treaties*, 2 vols (1938).

E. Mantoux, *The Carthaginian Peace* (1946).

H. Nicolson, *Peacemaking 1919* (1964).

A. Sharp, *The Versailles Settlement: Peacemaking in Paris, 1919* (1991). The most recent comprehensive treatment of the Paris peace conference, and has an excellent list of further detailed reading at the end.

Books on the 1920s

A.P. Adamthwaite, *The Lost Peace. International Relations in Europe 1918–39* (1980).

G. Egerton, *Great Britain and the Creation of the League of Nations* (1979).

C. Fink, *The Genoa Conference, European Diplomacy, 1921–1922* (North Carolina, 1984).

M. Gilbert, *The Roots of Appeasement* (1966).

R. Henig, *The League of Nations* (Edinburgh, 1973).

P. Kennedy, *The Realities behind Diplomacy* (1981).

M. Kitchen, *Europe Between the Wars* (1988).

S. Marks, *The Illusion of Peace. International Relations in Europe 1918–33* (1976).

G. Martel (ed.), *The Origins of the Second World War Reconsidered: The A.J.P. Taylor Debate after Twenty-Five years* (1986).

W.A. Macdougall, *France's Rhineland Diplomacy, 1914–24: The Last Bid for a Balance of Power in Europe* (Princeton, 1978).

J. Néré, *The Foreign Policy of France from 1919 to 1945* (1975).

G. Ross, *The Great Powers and the Decline of the European States System 1914–45* (1983).

S. Shuker, *The End of French Predominance in Europe: The Financial Crisis of 1924 and the Adoption of the Dawes Plan* (North Carolina, 1976).

M. Trachtenberg, *Reparation in World Politics: France and European Economic Diplomacy 1916–1923* (New York, 1980).

General Books on European Diplomacy

F. Gilbert, *The End of the European Era, 1890 to the Present* (1971).

J.A.S. Grenville, *The Major International Treaties 1914–1973. A History and Guide with Texts* (1974).

J. Stuart Hughes, *Contemporary Europe* (New Jersey, 1961).

J. Joll, *Europe since 1870* (Harmondsworth, 1976).

S. Lee, *Aspects of European History, 1789–1980* (1982).

J.M. Roberts, *Europe 1880–1945* (1967).

A.J.P. Taylor, *From Sarajevo to Potsdam* (1966).